Chapters

Introduction …………………..……………..2
1 - Waking up……………..…..……………..4
2 – Childhood ………....…….………....……7
3 – High School……....…………….………23
4 – The beginning of my end up North……..39
5 – Starting fresh…………...….…………...52
6 - After college…………….……....………73
7 - In my element ….…………….....………82
8 – Sunday 7th October 2012………....…….93
9 – Moving on……………….……………..108
10 – Rehab beggins…………….…………..111
11 – The "new Greg" and life today…….....200

Introduction

I was 22 years old and thought I was *invincible,* what young lad doesn't? I was soon to discover how wrong I was. In the early hours of Sunday, October 7th, 2012, I was the sole survivor of the 3 involved, I remained unconscious for the next 4 months, during the coma, my heart stopped completely on two separate occasions, my chance of survival got so low that, my family were advised to say their goodbyes. Following such devastating brain injury, it took years for me to understand what had happened and even longer to come to terms with my injuries.

Life since the crash, certainly is a tremendous amount more difficult, I'm completely physically incapable, I need carers round me 24/7 but, after finding the right mental attitude, I make it work. In writing this book, I'm telling my story, but I'm also passing on the message that **life is what YOU make it**.

Not only did I survive, but I also defied all odds in my recovery. Since the crash, I *have* become "new Greg". I've chosen to use the crash to my advantage, and I'm determined to make the most of the second chance I've been given.

Before the event, I had made some poor choices in life and was known to numerous police forces at both ends of the country. So, "why was I saved?" I'm now trying to justify this by 'giving back' in any way I can.

I'm desperate for redemption, the stories I share in the following chapters let you in on becoming the "old Greg"; the angry, nasty, aggressive young man who chose the wrong path and how I've managed to "handle" the adverse situation to my advantage.

I've chosen to share my story in the hope that, it could be of help to others, anyone who might need it, may be about to need it, know someone who might benefit from a little reassurance. I want to show you that, finding the right perspective can and will open many doors in life.

If you've only ever known me since the wheelchair, please don't think any less of me – everyone has a past, "some are more colourful than others", ok mine is illuminous, but I'm "new Greg" now, I'll only ever be that delightfully charming, bundle of joy you've no-doubt, grown-to admire. Those of you who knew me, knew of me, or dealt with me at some point in the decade before 2012 - there's a good chance I owe you one of these at least, please accept my most genuine, heartfelt apology.

"It's not the cards you are dealt in life, it's what you do with them"
I've written a book without even lifting a finger... 'just sayin'.

Chapter 1

Waking up

February 2013

I opened my eyes and the first face I focussed on was dad's.

I could not move; although puzzled this didn't bother me initially. My head busied itself trying to work out where I was. I couldn't even mentally answer some of the most obvious questions anyone in that scenario would ask themselves, "what's going on? Where am I? What's happened?" I was in a plain white featureless room; the silence was haunting. Once I had gotten my immediate baring's, the most intense metallic flavour took over my taste, completely engulfing the entirety of my sinuses.

The bed was against a wall to my left, there was a window, but the blinds were drawn. I could not see or feel any signs of injury on my body. From what I could see, there were no hospital machines, no plaster casts, no cuts, not even so much as a bruise, 'whatever was going on, whatever had happened, it can't be that bad, I'd remember, or at least be able to feel something surely?'

There were some more family members standing along the right-hand side of my bed next to dad; Jen (step mum), my brother Alfie, my Auntie Barbara and family friend Kathryn. The females in the room looked emotional, but in an excited kind of way? – which multiplied my confusion. I was too busy trying to make sense/think of what had happened, or at least work out where I was and what was going on, to pay real attention to them, they were cheerfully emotional, so I wasn't too concerned.

I remember the look of happy, excitement on everyone's faces, the first person to speak was Dad. In the calmest, most reassuring tone, he said to me, "Greg, you were in a bit of a bump in the car, you're being taken care of, you've been here for a little while, you're awake, you're stable, everything is good and we're happy to see you." Dad sounded his usual reassuringly neutral, calm, and collected self, "it can't be that bad?" I just could not figure out where I was, what had happened, or what was going on?

Obviously, I tried responding, but nothing came out? At that moment, my head was about to burst, 'I can't move, I can't talk, but physically I feel fine?' I was completely disorientated, even if I'd have been able to talk, my brain was not capable of piecing together a response, I just had a head full of exclamation marks. I just could not figure out what was so wrong or why I was there. 'I feel fine physically so why can't I move? Why can't I talk?' I understood the words Dad had just said to me but being totally unaware of the whole scenario, I was still oblivious.

Dad showed me an envelope, he began telling me "The results have arrived," I was still in the same bewildered state, but I felt like I had an idea of what he was referring too. Once I had been told what the letter said, I had the feeling that this was good news but, at the same time, this made little sense to me.

Looking back, I can think of plenty of relevant things that I should have thought and wanted answered, "was anyone else hurt?" "Am I injured?" "A bump?" "Was it serious?" "Why can't I feel any injury?" "Where am I?" Dad could see that the lights were on, but there was no one home.

Over the following week or so, I gradually built a very broken understanding of where I was, but I was still unaware of how much time had passed, the next milestone for me was learning the date.

Me and Alfie were watching tv one evening and the news came on. "Good evening, its blah blah February, here's your news", 'February?' Faint alarm bells started ringing in my head, followed immediately by frightening, confusion. I thought "strange, why are they saying February?"
I began frantically mouthing words, Alfie scrambled to pick up the card so that I could spell out a question. He confirmed the date and how long I'd been asleep. Moments after my brain managing to make some sense of what I'd just been told, I felt like I'd just been hit flat out by a fully loaded freight train, my whole world just crumbled. The penny dropped with the most deafening thud, that was the first I understood of the overwhelming magnitude of the whole thing, the reality was that I had been unconscious long enough for all the cuts, scrapes and broken bones to heel, the plaster casts had been removed. Unless paying close attention there was little to no visual sign that I had been injured, just scars here and there, which I couldn't really make out with my terrible new eyesight.
I had so many questions. Poor Alfie couldn't answer all my questions, or maybe he just didn't want to be the one to break the enormity of the event to me?

Chapter 2

Childhood
1990's

I was born on the 6th of September 1990, my earliest memories are of growing up on a farm "Mission Springs" near the town of Bawtry, I lived with Mum and Dad, my full sister Abi, and James, my older half-brother (same mum different dad).

For a small child the farm was a sort of wonderland. The farm itself was about 20-something acres but, in my eyes, the space was endless - fields upon fields that went on forever, I would spend my days doing whatever I wanted. Exploring, wandering, playing in the offices, barns, stables, and other outbuildings, I got up to all sorts. In the early 1990's, todays grave concern about health and safety wasn't such a thing then, but no harm came to me. The farmhouse was huge, there was 4/5 double bedrooms, my big brother James had the entire attic space, which had been converted and was now just 1 big room and there was a couple of residential apartments at one end of the outbuildings.

Because it was not a working farm, my mum was able to pursue her passion for horses, she had a dozen of them.

Unfortunately, Mum had started to develop a problem with alcohol. Mum was at home with the kids throughout the day, this enabled her to keep the new habit from Dad to an extent.

Things weren't good between them. I have memories of being on the floor in the kitchen and when they'd start arguing I would get between them and put a hand on each of them, whilst looking up, this would always stop them immediately, obviously it would have carried on, but not in front of me.

Mum's drinking had become a serious problem, so much so that my dad was pushed out of our home, and he went to live with his sister, my aunty Barbara. Mum moved on and met someone else, Mum's new boyfriend John moved in, my younger brother Jack, was born shortly after. I think James moved out around this time?

In an attempt to generate cash Mum started offering weekends of horse-riding lessons with accommodation, I have memories of strangers coming to stay in our house, after Dad had gone it just didn't feel the same.

After dad left, things became chaotic, everything on the farm started to "fall apart". I did not know the reason behind this at the time, I would notice that integral parts of the building, such as carpet and doors started to disappear. There was a giant brick-paved courtyard between the house and the offices, stables, and garages on the opposite side. One day there were no longer any bricks underfoot, leaving only the bare ground/sand underneath. Not that it bothered me - this was great for my little pedal tractor. Looking back, obviously these things were being sold – to raise some money.

Mum's new bloke would do various bits around the farm, but other than remembering his appearance, I don't really have any memories of him at all, good, bad or otherwise. I do have vague memories of attempting "family stuff ", walks, trips to play areas etc; but the walk would always end at the pub, and the play areas were always in the grounds of a pub. As time went on, mums' habit never stopped developing.

Mum started letting refugees set up camp on our huge lawn. Their massive marquee tents covered nearly half of the lawn. It was coming up to the mid 90's, I was a young child living in the Yorkshire countryside, I had never met or even seen anyone of colour before, their appearance was new to me, and they spoke a different language, so I was very confused, I was sort of intimidated, regarding our new visitors. Mum sat me down to "have a word", this was enough to clear up my confusion, putting my mind at ease completely.

By this time Mum was drunk pretty much all day most days so she was no fun. Her bloke was no fun either, from what I remember us kids were just left to do as we pleased. Kids are very adaptable and of course I had never known any different, so I just continued in my own little world.

I will never forget, a night when Mum had gone out, there must have been some event or occasion as I don't remember this happening any other time. It was past bedtime, and I was still up, showing off to the babysitter. I claimed I was hungry; next thing I'm sat at the table in the kitchen, I remember the babysitter clearly didn't want me to do what I was in the process of doing. I carried on pouring the cereal into my Peter Rabbit bowl, she was making a fuss? Something about the milk "yea whatever" I was showing off, I'll eat it anyway. I poured this milk on my cereal and started eating, after needing to chew a mouthful of the lumpy milk. "Oh…".

I had already started school; I must have been maybe reception or year1. Because we lived in the sticks the school would send a taxi, for me, Abi and 3 or 4 other kids off neighbouring farms, the journey was ok, right up until Hansen released 'Mmm-Bop'. Anyway…

I enjoyed school as any young child does, but due to each of my ears joining my head at $90°c$ (wingnut). I was ridiculed endlessly, being so young, I was equally sensitive; this would reduce me to tears most school days. Even though Dad didn't live with us anymore he still managed to find a solution, he arranged an operation for me to have my ears "pinned back". I can recall waking up after the op' to both of my parents stood next to my bed, both calm and totally civilised. This was the last time I ever saw them in the same place, at the same time.

The time came for us to leave the farm. I didn't know why we were leaving, I wasn't bothered, it didn't really matter to me, but now it's obvious that we would have been evicted. We moved to a small two bedroomed house on an estate closer to Bawtry in a much more built-up area, not exactly busy, simply having neighbours next to us, meant more built up. I shared a bedroom with Abi, Jack would sleep with Mum, downstairs most of the time I think, I don't ever recall mum using her room.

My older brother James did not move with us. Later I would learn that he had moved in with his dad. I loved the farm, but the move didn't bother me, I was so young, I didn't know what was going on. The way I saw it, my bed had simply moved. I was not mad or upset about the new place, there were a few big fields at the end of our road, so it really didn't feel that much different.

I started a new school; I remember this was where strangers began taking me out of class to "talk to me". I had no idea what it was about at that age, they would ask me about my home life, personal things like that. Looking back, they would obviously have been Social Services.

Our next move followed very soon after this one, the next move was to 27 Wellington Road, an address I will never forget - on what I called "The Prison Estate". In this second house since the farm, I shared a bedroom with Jack, Abi had her own room. By this point mum spent all her time on the sofa, her bedroom didn't even look like a bedroom, it was just a room, full of "stuff". I remember, our beds never had bedding, sheets, duvet covers etc, me and jack didn't even have pillows. There was no carpet in this house, the upstairs was just naked floorboards, downstairs was all solid floors. Being so young I didn't see this as even irregular, the only issue for me was that, as there wasn't any carpet on the stairs, all those needle-sharp carpet-gripper strip things around the edges of each step were uncovered, just as long as we had coins for the meter every time it ran-out, or just wasn't too dark naturally - these were no issue.

This estate was built around a prison HMP Lindholme. Our back-garden fence was no more than 5 metres from the tall grey prison fence. I have a lot of unhappy memories from time spent here, I was too young and unaware to be unhappy with "life" there and then, after reflecting on it so much over the years, it's easy to see that life wasn't great.

When we moved there, I was only 6/7 years old, a skinny little thing. Despite this, it was the kind of place where Mum could send me or Abi over to the shop for fags and/or alcohol with a note and they would happily serve us. The shop was only, maybe a couple of hundred metres away at the most, if you took the shortcut over the grass, between the houses. Not very far but, far enough to be a struggle, across the uneven, muddy ground, in typical cold, wet Yorkshire weather, when mum wanted a big bottle.

The new address also meant moving to a new school. This was Hatfield Woodhouse Primary, Mum's drinking was soon to be at its worst, I was being taken out of class to answer more and more questions about mum, home life etc.

Mum was flat out drunk most of the time. She was unpredictable. She might be perfectly fine, no problems, then she would flip and become angry at the drop of a hat. In her defence, I imagine she would have felt that her life was being/had been completely torn out from under her, so mentally I've no doubt she was already way beyond the end of her tether. Having 3 young kids to handle/cope with can't have helped, and no doubt exaggerated her frustrations, any problem tended to get blown way out of proportion. She could also be quite cruel; I don't think this was mum; the drink was doing this.

Like most young boys I was getting into football. I remember Mum coming with me, Abi, and Jack for a kick about on the playing fields near our house. I was in goal and every time I let a goal in Mum started tormenting me.
"Ya bum go home, Ya bum go home…"

(In a football chant kind of tune)

Jack and Abi were so young, they knew no better, and joined in. Eventually I ran off in tears.

A memory that stands out – by the time we had gotten off the bus and made it to the house it was already getting dark, so it must have been around autumn maybe? I had gotten into trouble at school again, I was playing with scissors in class. I started winding my mate up by snipping his way with the scissors, I found scaring him entertaining but then of course, the inevitable happened and I accidentally caught his skin. It was not a major injury, but he started bleeding, the school told Mum; she was angry. It would have been later in the evening, as I had gotten ready for bed (in my underwear). I was in the kitchen for something, as was Mum, she started shouting at me, working up an anger. After giving me a good beasting, she finished by shoving me out the back door.

It was dark and cold; I was stood there crying my eyes out. Unintentionally I/or the commotion made enough noise to disturb the neighbours, a couple of gay guys lived in the house next door. The back doors were on the sides of the houses, facing each other about 3meters apart, separated by a pathetic little picket fence. One of the guys came out and could see me stood there nearly starkers, bawling my eyes out, shivering and he offered me a coat. I said no, I was worried this would only aggravate Mum and make the situation worse.

One night, Mum was in her usual place, on the sofa in front of our black and white TV, when we went to bed. It had gotten late enough for all us kids to be asleep, Mum came upstairs to get us all up. She warned us to be very quiet, saying there was someone in the house. This terrified us, creeping all the way down those stairs in the dark, so obviously stepping on/catching our feet on a good few of those carpet strip things. She took us out the front door where there was gravel underfoot. I remember not being able to walk on it with bare feet, Abi was only 8/9 years old at the time but, she carried us, me on her back and little Jack on her front. Mum then woke a neighbour a few doors down, telling him there was someone in our house and asking him if he would go and check. He marched round there in his boots and underpants brandishing some sort of handheld tool, before coming back quite annoyed, confirming there wasn't anyone in there.

I have some good memories from that time, but they tended to be when I got away from home, on one of my little 'adventures'. I somehow had gotten a bike from somewhere and one day, I went off on my own for what felt like forever. I would cycle miles and miles exploring the surrounding area, obviously it wouldn't have been that far but, it felt it at 7 years old. No one was monitoring me/checking up on me, I would go out on adventures all day, every chance I got. I remember being round at a friend's house on the other side of the estate one day, this boys mum was fussing over me; "are you ok? Are you sure? Do your parents know where you are?" Of course, at such a young age, I did not find it strange that my mum was always preoccupied. I don't mean to sound critical; I'm just connecting dots. I don't think any of this would have ever been intentional, they say alcoholism is an illness and poor mum had it bad. Having a mum who was a serious alcoholic meant that I/we saw and experienced a lot of things that no child should ever have to. Yes ok, I know "it could've been worse" but, looking back it wasn't great. It seemed like most days there would be something that upset mum, it was easy to do something wrong. Experiencing some form of hostility was a daily occurrence. Dad tried again and again to get custody of Abi and me. He was aware that living with Mum was not doing us any good.

One day after school, as Abi and I were walking home from the bus stop. Approaching our house, we could see there were a handful of people walking up and down the side of our house, to and from the back garden. As we got closer and walked through the garden gate, we found Mum sitting in the middle of the grass, surrounded by strangers. I sat down next to her, Mum whispering, said to me, "I can see people up there in the upstairs window, but no one here believes me."

I remember to this day; I tried to convince everyone there that I too could see something/someone up in the window. Even though I couldn't, my instinct was to stick up for Mum, to take the attention away from her "surely, mum isn't the one who's wrong". Looking back, some of the people in the garden would've been more Social Services along with the relevant involved in the process that was initiated that day.

Following the incident above the authorities decided that, for the time being, Mum was not capable of taking care of us and Dad was granted temporary custody, it was now Mum's turn to do visits. Of course, we were completely unaware of all this.

The next move was to Chester. When Dad moved away, he went to live with his sister Barbara. Auntie Barbara (Babs) introduced Dad to Jenny, a fellow entrepreneur who owned a travel agents at the time. Things had developed and Dad now lived with Jenny and 3 of her four kids, Toni, David, Julie, and Rob, the youngest of Jenny's kids was 8 years older than me, they were all 2 years apart in age, the eldest had already flown the nest. The house was full, me and Abi, had bunk beds in the corner of the living room. Living in a family home was great!

Dad and Jen were a perfect match, Jenny sold her travel agency, and they went into business together – and had bought their first hotel, it was halfway up "Hough Green" – one of the main roads in and out of the city. Me and Abi moved in with Dad and Jen, on "Selkirk Road", 5-10minute walk from the hotel.

Dad and Jenny's hotel was called the Cavendish. There was a big kind of lounge room, at the front of the building, giant floor to ceiling bookcases ran right around the room, spread within the room were some very grand looking red button-back style sofas and a few matching armchairs.

There was a chessboard next to the windows, looking out the front of the hotel. Abi and I would spend hours just sitting there pretending we were playing chess; pretending we knew what we were doing. Whilst Dad and Jen were busy building their empire, there wasn't much for us kids to do. It was boring for us but, they had to work so hard to give us the standard of life they were going to provide us with.

With the move comes another new school, Overleigh St Mary's – We were only here very briefly. School was only a 10-minute drive, up the busy main road. As I said we were only there briefly, because Dad and Jen bought another hotel. The Brookside, on the other side of town. The basement level of the hotel was living quarters, that's where we lived. This hotel was no more than a 15-minute walk from Northgate Arena (Chester's main leisure centre/public pool at the time) this is where me and Abi spent a great deal of our weekends.

I was eight years old; this was now my 5th different address, and my 5th different school. This one was Newton Primary and was just a short walk along one of those converted railway line footpaths. It went directly to/past the school; I really enjoyed the little walk in the morning. This is where my behaviour in school began to go downhill. This is where being troublesome began, in my opinion, in a few months Dad would start, occasionally getting called into school.

A visit with mum had been organised, we'd been told that when the pre-arranged time came, Dad would run us into town where we would meet Mum at Chester train station, then take it from there. After all the changes in our life, we had so much to report back to Mum.

Unfortunately, around this time, mum had tripped and fallen. The result of this was an injury to the side of her face, this didn't sound that bad. So, despite this I was still picturing our first visit since we'd been taken from mum, in my head this was insignificant and changed nothing. Even though nobody had directly shared anything negative in terms of opinions, regarding mum or the situation. After reading attitudes and reactions, I can clearly recall forming an understanding that my mum had done something wrong, I felt that I should match other people's reactions and treat her accordingly. "For those of you who might need to know this - Kids absorb and remember much more information/opinions/experiences than you might realise."

Although Dad had kept us up to date with what was going on with Mum, obviously there is a limit on how direct you can be with children. Considering our ability/inability to interpret what we'd been told, the mental picture this painted in my mind didn't seem that bad but, we were both nervous; I didn't truly understand the severity of the fall, I don't know about Abi, but I know I didn't. Anyway, at least we still had a few days to prepare ourselves.

Several schooldays had passed since learning of mum's fall, as soon as we arrived home from school one day, Dad led us into his bedroom, this already felt very odd, Dad's normally always in his office when we arrive home. Dad sat down on the edge of his bed facing us and speaking very softly came straight out with it "your mum passed away earlier today".

I don't know what went through my mind, most kids would get emotional, or at least react in some way wouldn't they? The first thing I said to Dad was, "So, can I have tomorrow off school?" obviously I didn't understand what I'd just been told, that or maybe choosing to be ignorant, or not really caring perhaps? I don't know, but I remember thinking, "Day off school, nice."

It turns out that, the cut on mum's face was the fatal injury. Because she was a relentless drinker, naturally the alcohol had thinned her blood, a side effect of this was that the blood couldn't congeal, forming a scab to close the wound, which would have plugged the broken skin and stopped the bleeding. Thinned blood is incompatible with naturally viscous blood – eliminating the use of a transfusion, over the following few days she never stopped bleeding, inevitably her blood level got too low.

Clearly Mum had made some poor decisions, but I do not know anything of her side of the story, so I feel it would be unfair of me to judge.

When the funeral was coming up, dad did offer to take us but was hesitant as did not think that a funeral was a place for children, his protective instincts kicked in. As ever, Dad wanted to shield us from the upset.

Following this sorry development, my behaviour worsened severely. I was being rude to all school staff throughout the day, I started bullying this kid in my class called Lloyd, not even for any reason. I think I just chose to dislike him, as an excuse to vent my anger; I would go out of my way to find problems with this poor lad – these problems always either began or ended with some form of physical aggression from me. I remember getting sent to the headmistress and Dad getting called in once or twice. Busy though he was, Dad always made himself available.

A year or so later, Dad and Jen bought a 3rd hotel. Northophall Country House Hotel, this one was just over the border into Wales, about a 50-minute drive from the hotel in Chester. This was my favourite of their hotels, it was sat on the top of a hill completely surrounded by either fields or woodland, to me it was a castle. The front lawn was a field in itself, it was enormous and was almost fully enclosed by massive trees bordering most of the grass.

Dad and Jen were now right in the thick of their careers as hoteliers, the hotel business was unrelenting. Dad and Jen were often working from the crack of dawn, right into the evenings. Although flat out Dad and Jen made time where possible to take us on days out as often as they could. Or Dad would find the time to take Abi and me out for a little treat now and then, there was a McDonald's at the motorway services not that far away, at 9 years old Maccies was possibly the most exciting treat, that could ever be expected. I remember Dad would always ask whoever happened to be sat in the front if he could just "try our burger" – implying nothing more than a light nibble, but then dads "light nibble" was about a third of the burger. Just light-hearted fun, we all found this funny, dad would always make up for this by eating our gherkins for us.

This was where mum's death really hit me emotionally, in my opinion. This hotel was pretty much "in the sticks" meaning, spending time completely on my own was easily achievable – so was an often occurrence, I don't mean I was a depressed, emotional wreck. I just remember choosing to segregate myself to go and have a good cry, spending time alone with my thoughts always resulted in dwelling on my circumstances, why "my" mum had to die and trying to work out what "I" had done so wrong to deserve it. Naturally as I got older – my social habits/interests developed, getting between me and this phase.

The move meant starting another new school. I was now 10 years old; this was my 6th address and the 6th different school, this time in the little village of Northop Hall. I was now in year 5, another new school time to make more new friends. No problem, I was very familiar with this process by now. This school was the smallest I'd ever attended – there were no more than 60 pupils all together, years 5 and 6 even shared a classroom.

I'd made friends with some of the boys in the year above, Mike and Adam, after spending time with them outside of school, I met Mike's older brother and his mates. Every time we bumped into one of them, they'd be smoking. The idea of smoking became appealing to me around this age, simply because I'd seen the older boys doing it.

This would be where I encountered my first illegal substance. I was with a mate; we were in his Nan's garage watching his big brother and his mates. They were using this homemade device to smoke it; they called it a "bucket". They all had a couple of goes each, then they started trying to get me to have a go, I gave in, and I had a go. Honestly, I coughed so hard, I think an organ very nearly came up. About 30 minutes of intense coughing passed and this overwhelming feeling of sickness put me on the floor. I was too young to even comprehend what I had done. The result of this – a "whitey".

I had absolutely no interest whatsoever in the above. Getting my hands on a lighter was of much more interest to me, like most small boys I was fascinated by fire. I'd pinched a lighter from somewhere within the hotel and I took it with me into school the following day, I didn't have a plan I was just excited to show it off to the other kids, I think.

It was break-time, I went into the toilets on my own, my curiosity took over and I held the flame under one of the tissue dispensers. The flame went crazy so quick, far quicker than I'd ever imagined, I bolted away to the furthest point in the playground. The size of the playground reflected the size of the school so was equally small, anyway all the teachers knew that the only kid likely to do this was me. My Dad was called in, surprisingly the school did not throw me out, despite, starting a fire within the building, midday during full attendance. This issue got swept under the carpet, I didn't hear anything else about it anyway.

I was in Year 6 now, I remember that when the weekend arrived, me and a mate used to get the bus to a small town nearby called Mold. They had a market there every weekend, whilst exploring the market we discovered a stand that sold BB guns, "wow"! We as most young boys would, thought they looked incredible. I don't have a clue how I managed to get the money to buy one, but I did. Dad wouldn't of ever allowed me to have a BB gun, so I had to keep it hidden. Of course, I had the excitement of taking it into school the next day, inevitably it was literally minutes before I was caught with it. Teachers reacted to this, more so than setting the school on fire, as this was my second year here, they were most probably getting sick of the problems. Yet again Dad gets called in, his young son has done "something else".

Considering those incidents, I was not consciously trying to rebel or be naughty, I just wasn't afraid/didn't have a problem with doing things I knew I shouldn't. No one dared or encouraged me to start the fire or get the gun, absolutely nobody else was involved in any of these decisions, I just did not seem to have the instinct of avoiding trouble.

At one point I played for the local football team, even though the manager was a close friends dad, eventually I got kicked off the team. I'm not sure why, I can only imagine I was not an easy child to manage.

One day, Dad took me and Abi out in the car, no idea why or where we were going? We didn't know this area; we'd not been here before. Unbeknownst to us this was the village of Hawarden (Harden). He drove to the top of this hill on a very nice estate, and stopped outside a very big, very grand looking, detached house, with the biggest front door I'd ever seen. He told us that this was our new home! We could not believe it, in just a few years we had gone from grimy council estates, to living in nice hotels, now we had our very own house to live in. This drastic change in life felt amazing, before we moved house, I had a few months of year 6 left.

As the next academic year would be in secondary school, all year 6 kids from all the schools in the area would get to spend a couple of days at the secondary school, simply to experience how the big school ran – an "induction day". On the induction day, people who I'd never seen or even spoken to before knew my name, the name Greg Sumner had already started to become known. I remember going "up the field" with some of the older lads. Everyone knew that "up the field" was where the kids who smoked a certain "something", went to do exactly that. By the time we came back down from the field, everyone knew/assumed what I had been doing up there. During my induction day I'd unfortunately understood that deliberately misbehaving earnt recognition/notoriety, which seemed to result in popularity. "Oh dear…"

The start of the academic year came round, I was now year 7 and a student at Hawarden High School. Abi wasn't a student here; she went to a different school.

Chapter 3

High School
2001-2005

When I started, there wasn't a single other student that I knew in my form (class), nor was there anyone I knew from primary school in a single one of my lessons, I think this was intentional.

Right from the start there was tension between myself and teachers, they'd obviously heard my name and/or had been given the "heads up".

Most schools arrange a trip for the new Year 7's to meet each other, get acquainted make friends etc. My school took us on a 3-day trip to Paris.

On arrival at the hotel, we were split into smaller groups. My group had been put on the hotel's top floor, it must have been at least 5 or 6 floors up. We were all excited and busied ourselves checking out each other's rooms. I discovered that the bathroom window in my room was unlocked, so of course I started launching handfuls of wet tissue out onto the busy open forecourt below. Everyone found it hilarious, and I did it plenty of times. Inevitably before long there were complaints and teachers stormed in. This was the beginning of secondary school trouble.

I wasn't punished at the time, I understood that there would be repercussions later, but this didn't bother me.

The following day we went to Disneyland. At the gates, the teachers told us to go off and spend the day having fun. It was a typical hot,

Parisian summers day; so, I along with most others were wearing shorts and T-shirts.

One of the rides was a ferry trip around the site's manmade lake. Around lunch time me and a few friends joined the huge queue. It was peak season so, it was really busy, eventually we boarded the ferry along with plenty of the park's other visitors, everyone there was literally shoulder to shoulder.

There were signs all around the area we had just been queuing, and all over the ferry itself strictly forbidding anyone from going in the water, this was the most prominent, obvious, absolutely crystal-clear rule. A little over the halfway point of the ferry's journey, I turned to the group of new mates behind me, handed one of them my t-shirt, "Watch this!"

I launched myself off the boat into the water, to the astonishment of the many people watching. When my head emerged above the water everyone was looking at me – gobsmacked. I then swam back towards the shore in front of the woodland part of land, got out the water and made my way back towards the park. I had zero respect for authority, and I suppose the huge audience was probably a factor also. No one from the park collared me for it, and although the teachers found out about it later, much to my surprise "as they hadn't seen me do it, they weren't going to punish me", of course they believed this sounded like something I'd do but, hadn't actually seen me do it.

There were a few other incidents on that trip and by the time we got back to school, all the teachers were now well aware that "Greg was one to watch". Teachers' opinions had followed me from the primary school anyway, but now all the teachers *really* knew they had to keep an eye on me.

Year 7 had only just begun and I was already banned from all future school trips. I didn't care; I was just enjoying doing what I saw as "having fun".

I did well, in terms of learning and behaved in subjects where I had good rapport with the teacher. For example, in my first year, I had a passion for history, when it was taught by Mrs G. I never once even heard her raise her voice; whatever you wanted to know she had the answer. I loved listening to her because she made the subject interesting to hear. Then the next year, history was taught by Mr G, he had a different way teaching, he was very "old school" – if he could have whipped out a black board and seated each student individually, he would of. Only he was allowed to talk during each lesson, we were just being told information, or he would read for the hour, there wasn't any interaction - my love for history evaporated. The same thing happened with Technology. When design tech', was taught by Mrs A, it was great, she was everyone's favourite. Mrs A was on another level as a teacher. She was lenient, but nobody would abuse her lenience because everyone had so much respect for her. If I was in trouble for something, teachers in general would involve themselves, interrogate me and treat me accordingly, but she never ever would. As far as she was concerned, she took me as I was at that moment. She got through to me - but again when the teacher changed, my love for that subject dried up too.

As time went on, I got suspended more frequently, as well as getting into trouble in school, I was doing some very questionable things out of school.

With all the trouble I was getting into, my name was well known throughout the school. I can't remember how this began but, I kept being told about this lad in the same year thinks he could 'av me'. It was now the weekend and things had developed; I was now charging around the local areas to track down this lad. Eventually the search took me to Ewloe (You-low) - where he was from, and I found him on the park directly over the road from his house. So over I go, giving it the biggun. I grab him, tried getting him to the ground but as I was just skin and bones, he was much heavier set than me, so also considerably stronger too. I spent a few moments embarrassing myself, before he accidentally tripped-over a leg of a nearby swing set. This was totally unintentional, but anyway he's now on the floor so I jump on him, I spent the next 10-15 minutes or so, just repeatedly punching him in the face, only ever pausing to attract attention by means of tormenting him/making fun of the situation. I got bored/wore myself out, and let him get up, I watched him scurry back over the road to his house. After spending a few minutes lapping up the attention from the others that were there, I went over to his house for a cloth to clean his blood off my hands, I walked over to his house and knocked on the door, he answered. I told him "Get me a cloth," after wiping my hands I threw the cloth in his face, then punched him once more, square-on -flattening his nose, he hit the ground, and I scarpered, highly amused by the whole event. I am so ashamed of this, "I'm sorry S"; I have told you this simply to help illustrate my character.

Throughout my first year of secondary school, I spent most of my free time with a few lads from the estate where most of the areas well-known, individuals came from. When with this group, practically all our time was spent doing things we shouldn't.

Through various incidents resulting in police involvement, my dad had been made aware of this group, and he'd forbidden me from spending time with them. Dad did set constructive boundaries, but I was never going to take notice. I just abused his trust and would lie through my teeth.

I was now year 8, 12 years old. It was the summer holidays, the weather was warm so I knew there would be mates out and about all hours, the entire weekend. As I didn't want to miss out on whatever ended up happening. I lied to my parents, and said I was staying at someone else's house that night. The parents of the group I was with, would let their kids stay out all hours anyway, so they were ok. We'd been roaming around, causing havoc all night, it had gotten to the early hours. We were bored, so found ourselves up on the school roof this was a go-to activity to kill time, (this next bit was completely unplanned, I think?). Our exploration led us to sort of allow ourselves in, the police would call it "breaking-in", "tomato-tomarto".

There was an outdoor square area known as "the quad" that could only be accessed from within the building, or by going over the roof, so, over the roof we went. 3 of the 4 walls that made "The quad" were classroom walls, the 4th was a big set of very old, brittle, single glazed glass doors, the school's canteen was the other side of these doors. We climbed down to discover they had been left unlocked – "sort of". Our curiosity led us to let ourselves in, whilst we were there, we raided the tuck shop, and whole kitchen area in general, we rooted through every door we could open with some "light encouragement."

Of course, we were quite proud of ourselves, once the new week started, we had let a couple of close friends in on our secret, despite those fellow 12-year-olds being sworn to secrecy, somehow word travelled fast, and it wasn't long before the teachers caught on. It didn't take much of an investigation to pin our names to it, the police were already involved. This didn't seem to matter to the lads from the estate, their parents would always argue their child had done nothing wrong. My Dad was always on authorities' side after all, whatever they would tell him was always true. Back then North Wales Police had this scheme, a child's first 2 offences before the age of 16 wouldn't be officially recorded in the hope that the interaction would be enough of a deterrent to prevent any further offending. I hadn't even made it to my teenage years, and this incident used the last of those chances.

Ever since day 1 living with Dad, I've had a very nice upbringing, I want to make that clear. In my opinion dad and Jen always took the best, most constructive and appropriate course of action regarding disciplining me. The extent of trouble I was getting into was 100% all down to me.

I was now 13 years old; I had learnt the necessity of money and after understanding that Dad wouldn't give me money for nothing, I had to get a job. I started working at dad's hotel, the odd shift here and there as the 'pot-wash'. You would have thought I'd have gotten some kind of special treatment as the owner's son, but no, dad made sure I received exactly the same treatment and pay as anyone else my age - £3p/h he wanted "my working life to start in the real world".

My sister had joined army cadets with some of her friends, and after hearing about getting the chance to fire guns, I joined too, Cadet's was every Wednesday evening, here I would learn about true discipline and structure, I loved it, I took part in everything.

In the summer holidays we would go away on long trips, we would join other cadet regiments from around the UK - it was loads of fun. Living, eating, sleeping in barracks, as a soldier for the duration of the trip. These trips were full of competitions in sport, shooting, orienteering, camping, drill-practice, it was great, and a great use of time, much better than going around causing trouble with mates. On these trips we took on regimented armed forces life, making our beds perfectly, polishing boots, ironing our clothes, obeying orders. I was just like every other kid there, my reputation didn't follow me, to me that place was all about rank. Sadly, I just lost interest and before long, got bored of it, I'd tried everything that I found exciting/interesting so, it didn't really stimulate me anymore and I stopped going, my desire to hang around with my mates took over. My urge to always be the centre of attention was back and stronger than ever - being funny, tough, naughty, rude, unfair, unkind, abusive 'let's go', adding to the problem, I just did not know where to draw the line.

Now 14, to kill time on the weekends I wasn't working, me and my friends would get on the bus to Chester, and we would just hang around doing nothing for the day, until eventually returning home before town's nightlife got underway. I remember 1 of these trips, I've no idea who I went there with, but I'd bumped into a couple of familiar faces. K, and T.B, these lads were from a different area but attended the same school. I'd never hung around with them outside of school before. They were in the year above me and had a similar attitude towards, trouble, authority etc. That day, whilst in Chester, we were in the Grosvenor Precinct shopping centre, we had found somewhere to sit, and just watch the world go by.

Shortly after finding somewhere to sit, we noticed a lad nearby, on his own, he looked to be similar age judging by what he was wearing but he was much bigger than us, this lad was built like a man. Just pacing back and forth, pretending to look in shop windows but at the same time clearly making direct eye-contact every chance he got. He had spotted that we weren't from the area, this was a clear confrontation.

I just sat there and met his gaze, he didn't scare me, K who was sitting next to me, was looking down and nudging me, trying to get me to look away. The truth was I didn't care, I was fearless well, more so just stupid, I completely faced him, I was up for the fight, even though he would have thrown me round like a rag doll, I couldn't see that, in my head I was the biggest one there. Anyway, after seeing the confrontation unfolding security intervened and so nothing ever came of it. Months later we learnt he was known as "Packo", and was from the most notorious part of Chester, he was the ringleader of the lads from his area. Following this stand-off, he obviously went back and told his mates about what had happened. I had absolutely no idea at the time, but this little incident would work heavily in my favour in the next year or so.

Whilst in town with T.H on a separate occasion, just killing time like usual. We were waiting at the bus stop, smack-bang in the centre of town, making our way home. A mate from town 'Albi' was just passing and stopped for a chat, quite obviously heavily under the influence of something, he began tormenting this adult man waiting at the same stop, who'd clearly had a few drinks. Albi was much shorter than lads of the same age – despite this he would happily row with anyone. Eventually this man's patience runs out, he got up and floored Albi, then legged it. I must have been in trouble for something else around this time because I had absolutely no intention of involving myself in any way, shape or form, I remember thinking and deciding 'nah, better not...'. I was sat down at the bus stop; I wasn't even going to get up. T very half-heartedly gave chase, whilst continuously looking over his shoulder, calling me over and over again, "c'mon Greg! e can't be doin' tha, c'mon Greg c'monnn!". Following this light persuasion, I got up, and joined the chase, down the road, quick right, quick left, up a flight of steps, onto and crossing Chester's walls (Chester is a walled city). Arriving at some shady little spot next to Chester's cathedral, this bloke was out of puff so stopped, and turned to face us, I didn't know what else to do, so I drew back and punched him as hard as I possibly could – I hit him, he hit the ground, we legged it. Thinking about it, as I only weighed about 7 stone at this age, I am positive that my "as hard as I could" would probably have felt similar to being struck with a damp sponge. The guy probably just went down because it was the easiest way out, anyway 'that was that' we returned to the bus stop and got the next bus out of town.

Whenever not with friends from school, I'd be with the area's older group, I was smoking weed a few times a week, it was all they ever did to be honest. They had all left school by this point, only 1 or 2 of the group were employed or in college. I can't believe this now but, back then as a kid I sort of looked up to these lads. One of the unemployed lads, used to make a bit of money selling bits of weed. Back then for £40 you could buy an ounce of "rocky". From an ounce you could make a profit of up to £25 – providing each of your customers bought the smallest portion. Me and a mate from that estate got into selling a bit of this just to cover my own cost, after discovering how measly the effort to reward ratio was. Anyway, very soon I grew bored of this, just sitting round mellow af, talking and listening to the BS spoken amongst those there was boring to be honest, so that was the end of that, the end of buying my own anyway. In my mind a drug dealer was someone who could retire by the age of 30. I had been drawn to the idea of selling this by the thought of easy money, but selling "rocky", just wasn't worth the effort.

Anyway, having fun with mates came first. Around the second year of high school, a different group of lad's sort of integrated into our group, they were Matty, Jay, Anto, and Ben. These lads weren't really "up for" the illegal stuff, they were often in the vicinity when a lot of it happened but, they would just be observing, they were just typical young lads, more into kicking a football round and generally having a laugh.

I started to hang out with those lads a lot more, eventually more so than the other lot, and did all the normal dumb things you do at that age, drinking, smoking, partying, but at the same time, I had continued to build on my reputation as a bad lad. Even at just 14 years old around where I lived, I was known enough that when I went into one of the areas shops it was sometimes the case that the person on the till would know of me and would turn a blind eye to a bit of shoplifting - or would serve me for stuff, knowing that I wasn't of legal age. At this age I was now a waiter, a weekend shift began as waiting on staff working in the restaurant, but would end, collecting, cleaning, and restocking glasses until the "wedding do" came to its end, these always went on into the early hours.

That lad a few years older, known for selling bits of weed, lived on the same red-brick estate as me, by this point he was known throughout the area as the sort of "Del Boy of drugs", when I was 14, he would have been 17-18 years old. He drove a Vauxhall Nova which was a complete heap, but at that time to us "scally's" this was our idea of a nice car. He always had a spliff on the go, whenever he'd pass me, he would always stop to give me a lift. During the journey, he used to say things to me like "I've heard you're pretty handy Greg, I've heard for your age, you're the one" this was encouraging especially coming from him, this kind of recognition was what I had been working towards?

The earliest conviction on my criminal record happened Christmas eve 2004, so around this time/age. I got caught shoplifting, then 9 months later, the next recorded conviction was for ABH (Actual Bodily Harm), I can't even remember the 2nd of these incidents, even though the second is a pretty heavy charge, especially for someone so young.

By the time I'd reached year 10, most weekends consisted of Friday night's working till late in the hotel. Saturdays, began by getting an early bus to town to work 9-5 in a men's designer clothes shop in

Chester's city Centre, then I would get the bus home, have some dinner, before ending my day by completing a shift at the hotel. Sundays, another early, cold, grim start, to catch an awkward "Sunday bus" in time to be in Chester's City Centre to work 10-4. There were two sides of my nature. One side was ambitious and wanted to 'do well' like Dad, fueled by Kanye's 'Hey Mama.' On the other side unfortunately, a more prominent side normally always heavily doused in 'Joop,' wanted to 'have fun,' driven by my immature, misguided desire for attention, regrettably, the most efficient way of doing this would be through misbehaving, pushing boundaries way beyond what was acceptable. The opening couple of lines of this paragraph sound good but the criminality hadn't disappeared. I had devised a way of concealing pieces of brand-new clothing, within the shops waste – in the clear bin liners, I would then put the rubbish out for collection, then get a lift to go and retrieve the items later that night. No one would have ever suspected me of such dishonesty, appearing as the decent, honest, hard-working type came easily, enabling me to maintain a 'wolf in sheep's clothing persona.

Around this time, my behaviour was nearing the worst of my school years, I'm sure some of the teachers probably assumed I was stupid but, considering by this point, I'd missed a good chunk of each academic year, I did OK, in terms of getting a decent grasp on a good range of subjects. If it was ever there to begin with, by this point, I had completely lost any interest I ever had in learning/being at school, it was just somewhere I went during the day to socialise. I'd only been there for 4 school years intermittently, and things had continuously worsened, they were running out of options of what to do with me.

Something had happened in school, nothing I hadn't done before – but enough to get suspended, therefore Dad had to be called in. On this occasion it was the deputy head (Mr. E) who called Dad to let him

know I needed to be collected. Mr. E had a very nice convertible Morgan car, Dad had picked up on this, on one of their many encounters. Dad knew by now, this man never passed on the chance of talking about his Morgan. During the commotion of getting seated, Dad mentioned "I prefer the E Type..."
Mr E dismissed this immediately and replied, "We need to talk."
– oh...
Me nor dad hadn't heard this stern kind of response before, must be serious. This would be the day that the school had decided to use their 2nd to last resort. The last option being to throw me out altogether.
I was sent to Llewyn Onn, Behavioural Unit in Hollywell, North Wales - which was known amongst staff and students as 'The Unit'.
The day I was taken to The Unit, another lad from a school a few towns over (in an area where I was known and dangerously unpopular) was also being sent there, we travelled there in the same vehicle.
It was the very first time we had ever met, the whole journey (about an hour) he sat there, telling me all the crimes he'd ever committed, fights he'd had, went into great detail about everyone he knew, all the well-known names that would back him up, obviously trying to let me know what a 'big deal' he was.
He wouldn't have seen me as a threat physically, like most - he was clearly bigger than me. I think he wanted to let me know just how bad he was.
Finally, we'd arrived, we both got out, I called him over "ey come ere" he walked over, and I immediately launched my hand at his neck, grabbing him by the throat. I'm not sure what I was intending to do, I wasn't really a fighter, but I thought I had better do 'something' – I didn't want him or any others there thinking that I wouldn't react. A moment passed - long enough for me to give him a good mouthful

before, his knee shot up, connecting firmly with my undercarriage. Embarrassingly, apart from surprising me, it didn't hurt a single bit. I was only 14 years old (that's my excuse); It gave me enough of a shock that I let go, seconds before staff pounced on us.

I had heard a lot about "The Unit" but, once I got there it was hard to see what all the fuss was about. It was just a tired old run-down building in a dreary place called Holywell next to an even more miserable place called Ryhl (dreary and miserable back then).

It was just somewhere to put difficult kids, to get them out the way. It didn't matter what you did, said, threatened to do, or who you said it too, staff just stood there and took it. I was not interested in being reformed, even if any effective effort had been made to do so. For me it was just unbelievably boring. I was at "The Unit" for about 9 months, there or there abouts, before the system had decided that they had done their job, and it was now time to start reintroducing me back into mainstream education.

The teachers were expecting some sort of transformation following my time at the "The Unit", there was a mild change, not quite the change the school had hoped for, I think it was just that teachers seemed to have a higher tolerance. Before long, my behaviour was just the same as it used to be.

It was hard to believe that I had made it all the way to the final year. Either my dad's constructive reasoning, or because they could see I had half a brain; I was still there. I reckon I *could* have done well, but I just didn't have absolutely any interest in doing so. My Dad had done an amazing job of talking me out of a lot of situations, whilst actively working with the school trying to get through to me, but they'd had enough. The trouble gradually worsened, they did let a lot of trouble pass, then after pushing them to their end, they'd had enough. GCSEs were just around the corner and "for the benefit of other students", they finally decided to kick me out. But Dad didn't want "expelled" to be recorded on my school record, he managed to talk them down, to "permanent study leave".

Marking me down on the register as being away on "study leave", meant I didn't have to be on the schools' grounds. The only conditions were

1. I mustn't ever be on or near the premises, unless instructed for an exam.
2. I mustn't be at home either.

The answer was to find some form of work.

I was perfectly content with this new arrangement, but this really upset Dad, he had tried every way imaginable over the years, hard, soft punishment, every penalty he could think of, in depth talks, anger, utter forgiveness, nothing worked – even though I'd brought about this decision, seeing what I'd done to Dad got to me. I solemnly swore, convincing both him and I that I would make a good go of this unique opportunity, that I'd get a job, and that I would get some valuable work experience, not just hanging about aimlessly with mates – not that he would've ever allowed that. I wasn't just saying this to comfort him, I truly meant it there and then, this was still of no real comfort whatsoever. At the same time, I was selfishly quite happy with this new arrangement, I wasn't sure but, this kind of felt like I'd reached my end goal?

So, I had effectively left school but every now and then I was meant to go in and take an exam. I was bright enough, and I could see the value of getting at least some GCSEs, but by that point in life, the only things on my mind were making money, girls, and having 'fun'. My life would turn so chaotic over the next 18 months that I only sat a couple of exams. They were both 2-part exams, and as I only did 1 of the 2 parts, I got no GCSEs at all.

There was a well-known guy in the area, he was a plumber. He was known for always driving nice cars. He seemed much older than me, but he was only 18/19. I proposed the idea of taking me to work with him - he had heard a lot about me, I think he quite liked the idea of having Greg Sumner working with him. So, he started taking me to work, thereby satisfying the "study leave" criteria.

This was meant to be the beginning of my career; I was going to be a plumber. We did what is called "first fix", fitting the plumbing into brand new houses, as they were being built.

Around this time, through a friend of a friend, I'd been put in touch with someone, mostly known for his incredibly volatile, aggressive, ferocious character, but also for selling something in particular. I'd started to dabble in "couriering", to begin with. The guy would ring me up. "I need you to take this to that person," I would get lifts from wherever I was - to him to collect – and then to the 'drop', I was just doing some of his legwork. The money earnt for just a few hours work, was nothing but fuel to the fire of my criminal ambition. I'd be on one of my two phones for pretty much most of the day nearly every day.

Soon enough I lost whatever interest I ever had in plumbing/working altogether, the money I'd started making on the side was both stupidly easy and much more exciting.

Then, a lightbulb moment, "I wouldn't need to pay out for lifts if I drove". I bought a little Suzuki Baleno, it was a 1.6 and far too quick for me, inevitably this car only lasted me a few days. My inexperience got the better of me and I crashed it – nothing serious, nobody got hurt, I've absolutely no idea what happened to the car, I didn't care anyway, I had much more going on.

The first few months with the most notorious guy, things were going well, he was setting up nearly all the initial deals, all the people I was sent to were always considerably older than me, well into adult life. They must have had plenty of money considering the venues I went to "drop" at and the amount of "call backs" I'd get.

Dad had been working every hour available for the last 48 years and was approaching his retirement, his plan had always been to retire once I had finished school. One day he hit me with it, "Right, where would you rather live after your exams; this place in Kent or this place in Kent?" I didn't want to move to Kent. I'd dedicated the last 7 years to making a name for myself, my notoriety was nearly at its peak. I did not want to leave the area and everything I'd set up, so very selfishly I dug my heels in.

Eventually, I/we came up with a solution: as my sister Abi was now 18, on paper she could, be my "responsible adult". She had already finished her time in education, she was employed, she worked at MBNA at the time. We both fancied it, so it wasn't just me going over and above to show Dad how ideal the idea was.
I was relentless, I never gave Dad a break, constantly going on about how much of a practical solution this would be and how I/we could and would manage, no problem. I wanted this so badly, the stakes were that high I was an absolute saint, always home on time, always doing absolutely everything Dad ever asked of me, and even proactively doing whatever else I thought he might've asked for, so there wasn't even anything left for Dad to want done. Because I was no longer at school, Dad stopped getting all the letters, report cards, phone calls, this was a first, I think that this indirectly had a positive impact. After months of faultless, exemplary, unspoiled behaviour, Dad reluctantly agreed to rent an apartment in Chester for us.
As my sister, Abi didn't have enough control over me, unfortunately it would be too late by the time we made this realisation.

Chapter 4

The Beginning of my End up North
2005-2007

I want to make it clear that I am incredibly ashamed of my criminal past and if you think I am at all bragging about what I got up to then you are missing the point completely. Everyone has a past; some are more colourful than others, if I am going to tell my story effectively, I need to say enough to give you an understanding of my character and personal life, that means detailing certain aspects. If anyone questions for even a moment whether the path, I took was the right one, the answer should be clear. I would also like to point out that, of all the people I've known over the years, who've tried the criminal path, some get further than others but, not one of them has benefitted from it long term, several are dead, a handful are serving long sentences at his majesty's pleasure, and 1 is still on the run today. (2024)

This idiotic idea would be the beginning of the end for me as far as my life in the North was concerned.

Throughout secondary school, I would develop and lose a fondness for a variety of "the typical" substances tried by many teenagers/young adults.

Since just before my mid-teens, I was edging closer and closer to the idea of using drugs to make an income. The couriering had done an effective job of showing me just how easy this line of work appeared to be. I decided I was ready and competent enough to start doing it for myself. I started off buying 10 individual wraps ready for sale. If whoever didn't have the money for their order, they would take it "on tick', meaning they'd pay when their money came in.

The guy I got the product from was the most well-known and feared character in this line of work, throughout the surrounding areas. He was in his late 20's, full of muscle and covered in tattoos, his appearance matched his reputation perfectly. Everyone knew him and no one would ever dare cross him, ensuring those who took it "on tick", always paid up.

I never had any trouble regarding territory etc, if you were not a fighter people needed to know that you were in touch with the sort of people who could sort your troubles. Everyone knew that I was in tight with my supplier, so I was never challenged.

My supplier would always remind me "don't get high on your own supply," and I stuck to this rule rigidly. After a few weeks of earning, I wanted more so, I started to buy more. He would give me an ounce "on tick". Once tabs I owed and owed to me had all been squared up, I'd have a decent wedge of cash, I would spend it as quickly as I made it.

I would blow it on rubbish. I would get taxis here, there, and everywhere for me and friends, I would pay for meals out for us all, my wardrobe was packed with designer clobber.

Before long, I'd stopped spending time with my regular friends, and I'd gravitated towards the biggest, baddest crowds I could find, who were always much older. I was a bit of a drifter to be honest well, I had what a lot of people wanted so everyone was trying to be my mate – endless invites on nights out, parties, absolutely any social occasion, you'd be surprised.

Around this time my good mate Paj, invited me to a party at her house just outside of Chester, I made sure I'd be there after finding out who else was going. The group from the most notorious, part of Chester. Ever since I started at secondary school in North Wales, I/others in the area would often hear wild things about the craziest sorts of events, occasions, and characters from this place.

On this occasion there was 7 or 8 lads from that group, and guess who their obvious alpha was. Remember the big guy I nearly had a row with, in Chester City Centre a year or so ago? Yes – him.

I went along by myself; they were already there when I arrived. I just sat in my chair quiet, all night, intending to give off a strong silent sort of vibe. No idea if it worked, they probably just thought I was a bore.

After this I started spending more time with this group, because they were my sort of lads I had absolutely no problem integrating into this group, I think that my most current line of work, the people I knew, was known by and my general lifestyle bought me a fair bit of credibility, that coupled with not backing down to their alpha that time, I had some genuine respect from the group. By this point, I had gained a name for myself. I was known in most parts of Chester, an unhealthy ego boost for a child who feels like an up and coming "Teflon Don". I'd made a few enemies by this point too, but because of the people I associated with and what people heard, there wasn't anyone who'd act on their thoughts, or even make their feelings known, not to my face anyway.

Business was going well, so well that I got a phone call one day – from the areas 2nd most well-known name in this line of work, I had been headhunted. He said he would send someone to pick me up, one evening, I was collected in a brand-new BMW, then taken to some restaurant/diner place out the way. It had to be "out of the way" because this guy was actually "on the run" when we first met, anyway he wanted me to start shifting for him, at first, I turned down the offer, over the coming weeks he kept asking but my answer never changed. Being in close contact with both these guys felt like I must be doing something right, unfortunately a direct result of this meant my aspirations kept developing.

This was the only person I ever knew, brave enough to step on my guy's toes, so I assumed that he was of equal significance. Over the next month or so, more conversation and plenty more requests, I gave in. Soon, I would learn this was a big mistake, I discovered that although this guy's very well-known name made him seem equally as infamous, he wasn't anywhere near as feared or respected. People were much more relaxed about paying me, there was also a dramatic drop in the standard of clientele.

The people the other guy put me in touch with, normally always paid there and then, money was never an issue. New customers were always short or waiting on a payday.

I remember taking advantage of some poor bloke one night, he was easily at least 5 years my senior. I knew how badly he wanted what I had, he'd already spent all his money quite some time before this point but obviously, he still wanted more, I agreed to do it "on tick", providing he would buy me a couple of tickets for an 18-30's trip to Ibiza. He agreed!

That trip was eventful to say the least. The general nature of the trip, at the age I was, along with the interactions with females who were always older and despite being made aware of my age, were rarely deterred. This meant when returning; getting onboard the plane along with my ego was a very tight squeeze.

Once I got back, I continued working with the new source, everything was just like before Ibiza in terms of moving the product. There was no problem getting rid of it, but paying for it became an issue. I was too young and far too ignorant to realise that these people only wanted to be my mate to get some of what I had. Soon, my lifestyle got much, much bigger than me. People grew more and more relaxed about paying me, my personal use was now too much, and a lot of people were stitching me up in terms of debts being cleared, so I was slipping behind with payments. Over the next few months, I'd start working for/with a few different sources, "robbing Peter to pay Paul" sort of thing. This was totally unsuccessful, I simply kept adding to the list of people I owed money too. Most of the people within my reach and worth knowing in this line of work, knew of me, and no one would give Greg Sumner anything to sell because they knew I wasn't good for the money. I was struggling, the lifestyle I had been living was slipping away and never stopped gaining momentum.

I would do what I could to put distance between myself and "that life". I would chop and change between a couple of well-known groups between Chester and North Wales.

The North Wales group were from an area not far from where I used to live. I was the youngest of this group at 16 and the oldest must have been about 21, I think. These lads were always in the middle of some imaginative get-rich-quick scheme, very few of which went to plan and even fewer paid off! There was only one that paid off for me personally, a guy within the group knew enough about this "place" to become a problem. Being mindful of not going into potentially harmful detail for those involved - long story short I ended up with a brand-new ford fiesta. This would be my main mode of transport for the time being. Things often got boring, tedious, or just plain desperate with this group.

When not with the above, I'd be with the Chester lads, these were all like-minded, none who'd ever done the same as I'd been doing, but the concept of my recent line of work was by no means unheard of, to any of this crowd.

I had much more success in the Fiesta, in terms of keeping all 4 wheels on the road. I'd drive anywhere and everywhere; my ringleader mate of that Chester group got this vehicle "double plated" for me. Effectively making the vehicle invisible to police so, the fact that I had no license and was driving a stolen car never even registered as any sort of concern in the slightest to me personally.

I'd just mooch round, between Cheshire, the Wirral and North Wales doing bits 'n' bobs – giving lifts, killing time but, mainly scoping out different areas, trying to find/come up with something profitable. Also, helpful because whilst out and about, no one I owed money too could find me. I would regularly receive phone call's making sure I was ok and letting me know where not to go, spontaneous police roadblocks were popping up around familiar areas, random black fiestas were being pulled over constantly.

My schools' leavers prom for the year 11's was on. Ignoring my common sense, I had what I *thought* was a great idea, 'I know, I'll drive me and my mates there!' I did exactly that, upon arriving, parking, and making our way towards the events entrance, we were all refused entry. A couple of days after this, I'd just arrived home, on my own, around early afternoon I think, I'd just called in to get changed or something like that. One of my phones started ringing, it was Packo, "you home? look out your window", I looked out my kitchen window and saw nothing but police, filling the carpark behind the building where I lived. Honestly, I was bricking-it, waiting for them to come through my door at any moment, the car was being recovered. They never even came in the building as far as I know –

good job, 'ard man Greg' didn't have a clue what to do, I was shaking like a leaf. Anyway, the police left.

I didn't get physically arrested for that instead, I received a letter letting me know, I was being called in for an interview, along with a station, date, and time for me to attend. Because I was under 18 years old, I had to have an "appropriate adult" with me for the interview so, Abi accompanied me.

A copper came in the interview room alone, clearly, quietly confident that he wouldn't have any problem getting a child to "fess-up", I had my story ready, something I dreamt up – it was so obvious that I was lying, I told him "I'd been in a local chip shop one night and there was some bloke on his phone having a heated conversation about selling a car. The deal was obviously falling through, so I went over and said, "I need a car", the bloke answered - "great - I've got a car for you, a brand-new Fiesta - hundred quid." The copper knew full-well that I was lying, it was so obvious, but he didn't have the proof he needed to convict me.

My story was complete fiction. I knew it, he knew it, anyone who would have been listening would have been able to tell but, as he didn't have any evidence to contest my story, I just sat there intentionally appearing relaxed, slouched in the chair, arms folded smirking - that was the end of that. "Stupid little boy, who did I think I was!"

This really wound him up, he was on his feet by this point, his questions, actions, volume and tone had gotten quite aggressive. I think he felt a bit silly that he'd not 'got me', he properly lost his rag.

After a month or so following an investigation, I learnt that I would only be charged with "handling stolen goods and driving without a license or insurance." For which I received a driving ban and had to complete a "Y.O.T course".

No matter who with or where I spent my time, that massive issue of debt meant constantly looking over my shoulder, this concern was all day – every day.

This along with the endless concern of imminent backlash was all getting a bit much for me, I needed something to take up my time and distract me from the utter mess that I had made for myself. My mate Col' had recently been released from prison, within days he had a job and was at work most days, whilst talking one day he was telling me about his job. This got me thinking, 'Hmmm, that would effectively keep me occupied and out the way'. A couple of days of this idea floating around in my head passed, before telling him to get me a job there too.

 I was now a door-canvasser. Attempting to sell the fantasy of double glazing for a national home improvements company. This worked for me as my workday would involve being driven to a random location, always outside of Chester and just spend the day walking round, knocking on doors, talking to strangers. This job wasn't to earn money, it just gave me something to do each day. Whilst there, the senior team leader Adele, who was 2nd in command, she must have been about 4 years older than me. She was an avid Liverpool supporter and one weekend she arranged a bit of a trip for staff, to nip over to Liverpool to watch the game. She brought along her younger sister Kylie, who was a couple of years older than me. I was an absolute stunner at 16 years old, we got chatting, obviously I blew her away and we started going out. A short while later Adele started going out with a lad who worked for the same firm, Wayne. He was exactly my sort of bloke, we were very alike in terms of criminal involvement, he was a few years older than me, he was in much-

much deeper than I was, he had just been formerly relocated from Manchester after serving an IPP sentence.

After we got to know each other a bit, we hatched a plan to make some money. We did consider sticking with the same product but mutually agreed against it as the higher value stuff, is always higher risk too.

So, we decided to try our hand at shifting copious amounts of a different item. Individually these little things sold for just £2 each, but we were selling them in 'packs' (multiples of 500). I was making a great deal less than I'd been making previously but, a great deal more than I had been door canvassing.

I understood that he had some serious contacts, this was obvious as he had such ease getting hold of huge amounts of whatever. A week or so after first meeting, he told me he had a gun, he had it buried in a patch of woodland/wasteland next to Chester City's football ground, I've no idea why but I talked him into letting me have it for a bit, we went and got it. I had heard from someone, "the gun on its own is 10 years custodial instantly, and each live round was worth an additional 2 years", thinking with my sensible head – "better stay away from bullets then" – "yeah, that's obviously the most sensible way to have a gun, good thinking Greg. Idiot!"
I had trouble finding the right words, to explain that. I struggle to understand where I felt I was mentally, at that point in life. The reality of just how much trouble I could get into, would only ever flash through my mind very occasionally and even then, only ever briefly. I would "borrow" or "look after" this quite often, not for any reason – just to have it.
I lost touch with Wayne pretty much as soon as I left Chester. Kylie got in touch a couple of years ago to let me know, Wayne sadly passed away (2022) – rest in peace mate.

A much-needed wakeup call regarding the gun came along with a visitor one day. This unplanned visit took place coincidently, just a couple of days after Abi had found it in our flat. Abi's discovery really frightened her, scarier than finding a firearm in her home, she was terrified by the thought of what her little brother was involved in. I sat down in the armchair facing this visitor completely oblivious, as to what they now knew. Our flat wasn't at all big, so even though we were sitting on opposite sides of the room, we were still within each other's personal space. "You have a gun, Greg?"

I knew that this person had been in countless, difficult situations throughout their life, so they were well experienced in maintaining an appropriate reaction. I could see that the individual was trying their hardest to keep it together, but this topic of discussion was too much, it completely broke them, halfway through hearing my cagey, inconsistent response, I could see tears in their eyes. When I saw that, it destroyed me, knowing that I had reduced this person to tears, was a knife through my heart. Of course, at this age "I thought" I was an expert at lying effectively, I protested that "Abi was a liar, talking a load of "shid"! This person always wanted to believe the best of me, and they swallowed it, I got rid of it within the hour and swore to myself, that would be the last time I would ever have anything to do with it. I hate to admit it but, due to my world imploding, my desperation meant I would fail to keep to my word on this but, those stories are not for this book

Looking back now "what the FLUK was I doing!" who did I think I was?! 16 years old, casual crime, stolen cars, class A's, and firearms. What was I playing at!

Adding again to the feeling of this life I'd created, being obliterated, one day my sister rang me to say that our flat had been broken into, and anything of any value had pretty much been cleared-out. This was someone that I owed money too, someone I'd tried working with, dropping by to "have a word". (I know exactly who it was, I just don't want to give him any recognition)

After the raid I thought it would be unwise to return to the flat, so I was now sleeping at my girlfriend's house in Blacon, her mum knew about the trouble I was in, she didn't say anything about it, other than warning what she would do to me, if her daughter came to any harm. By this point, I felt that I couldn't really go out if not in a vehicle. Things were bad, and of course my closest friend at the time had the gun, I started asking myself "what am I playing at?" After the next couple of incidents involving the gun, I felt that my time in the North of the country had come to its end, I needed to get away, a new sense of urgency to get out of Chester had developed.

I have some siblings in Somerset, James and Anna-Marie (same Dad, different Mum). Everyone knows James as "Alfie", so I'll call him "Alfie" from now on, so you don't confuse him with the other half brother of similar age, who I lived with on the farm - also called James (same Mum, different Dad). Alfie and Anna-Marie are both around a decade older than me.

We spent a fair bit of time together on the farm years ago, but we hadn't seen a great deal of each other in person since, we would see them at big family occasions weddings etc, and maybe speak on the phone at Christmas but that was about it.

I contacted Alfie and told him about my troubles, and he drove up to collect me as soon as he could. Since my flat had been cleaned out, when Alfie arrived to pick me up, I pretty much just had the clothes on my back and a little wrap of green. When I got into his van I began "skinning up", I soon realised I'd forgotten my measly cling film wrap, so I quickly let Alfie know and asked him to turn round – he said "ahh use mine" and chucked me a sandwich bag full of it. "Haha my saviour!"

Over the coming years I was often startled by just how alike we were, the most obvious likeness was that our sense-of-humour's matched perfectly, our imaginations, social preferences, hobbies, interests, - all so scarily similar. Despite the massive age gap and the fact that we hadn't ever lived together, or even spent much time around each other, we were so alike. People doubt that we're actually related because I'm much more attractive – but the similarities between our characters were uncanny! He took me to live with him and his girlfriend in a little village called Winscombe in Somerset.

Like all dad's kids, Alfie's hunger to do well was clear and he had his own delivery business, at the time he was distributing bathrooms nationally.

A typical day in the beginning of my life down south; Alfie and I would be up at 4.30am, we would be out all day and would aim to get home around 4pm. The first 6 months or so, my time in Somerset blended into one, it was great. I would go everywhere with Alfie, and we would share stories continuously, Alfie was hilarious. As I've said we had seen each other on family occasions weddings, the occasional birthday over the years. But it wasn't until this point that we first understood just how alike we were. I'd never had a relationship with my big brother before, mentally, I went from being the lad that needed to be known, to just being known as "Alfie's little brother" and that was fine by me. My desire to be known just completely vapourised.

I was completely in awe of him, he couldn't go anywhere without being known. Everyone knew him, and everyone loved him. This was exactly what I wanted to do up North – kind of, but he'd done it more effectively than I'd ever seen it done before simply, just through being a decent bloke, that everyone found hysterical. Somewhere along the line I developed the understanding that being a tough guy, funny guy, naughty guy, or the flash guy earnt popularity. I had fulfilled all these roles at different points, but without respecting that each had its limits/boundaries. I had achieved notoriety up North but for all the wrong reasons, whereas Alfie was so widely known simply through being the most entertaining guy in whichever room he happened to be in.

I can think of no better way to convey how much love and respect I have for my brother than by telling you that my eldest son is named Alfie.

For the time being, I was happy that no one knew me, I could go out without looking over my shoulder. There wasn't anyone looking for me down South. When I first moved down there, I kept seeing old faces of people I owed money too, but this was of no great concern, I had my big brother with me now.

Chapter 5

Starting fresh
2007

It was 2007, I hadn't yet turned 17. I was now living with Alfie in Winscombe. Things started well; my big brother was my new idol; he was well-known and well-liked. I looked up to him so much, I started trying to sound like him, dress like him, I would do whatever I could to imitate him.

Alfie knew about the trouble I had been in up North; it wasn't anything he hadn't heard done before; nothing ever shocked or surprised him. Generally, he would sort of laugh it off or advise me on how I should have done it. I'm sure he would have tried "having a word" but he knew full well, the sort of character, at the age I was, absolutely nobody could've ever gotten through to me, or have even gotten me to listen to anything constructive, regarding my behaviour, personality or future. He knew it would have been a complete waste of time, effort, energy, and breath. He knew this as he had the same attitude to 'trouble' at my age. Instead, he was just a great role model - someone who worked hard and got on in life, Alfie hadn't always stuck to the straight and narrow, but he'd learnt from every experience over the years, whereas my criminality just kept snowballing.

When I escaped Chester, Anna-Marie, handled everything regarding my most recent encounter with the law, and got the case transferred down south where it was taken on by the local Y.O.T. (youth offender team). Anna-Marie is amazing, almost a second mother figure. I'd never lived with her either, but she's someone who is always on the end of the phone and ready to help in any way she can. To this day, if I can't get hold of Dad, she's the person I'll call next.

The office for the local youth offender team was in Weston-Super-Mare, I had been summoned there for an introduction, Alfie gave me a lift there, he was my "appropriate adult" on this occasion. We were sitting in the waiting room, and I was aimlessly flicking through their leaflets, reading bits here and there. I got called into a room with 4 or 5 other lads, each of which were in the same scenario as far as being sentenced to attend the Y.O.T's meetings. The bloke in charge started things off by asking "does anyone understand why they're here?"

I stuck up my hand and basically just recited what I'd read moments before in one of those leaflets. Honestly, the guy nearly fell off his chair, he was blown away; he had never heard such a perfectly, precise, articulate response. I managed to do this a couple more times in the meeting and right from the off, he had me down as a star pupil. As soon as Alfie and I got out the door we both burst out laughing, we were in stitches, Alfie could see exactly what I'd just done. I know I probably should have taken it more seriously, buuut…. As a result of becoming "model student," I was awarded the following few sessions to be home visits, after maintaining my productivity I got the course cut in half.

The driving ban, much to my amazement and delight, would run concurrent with my age at the time of conviction. As I was only 16 at the time, this meant that by the time I was 17, I would be allowed to get my license legally.

After turning 17, I took my driving test and sailed through it, Anna-Marie and Alfie bought me my first legal car, a Ford Escort. Being on the road legally was a whole new experience, to begin with my eyes were always fixed to the rearview, always on the lookout, old habits die hard. This car didn't last long at all, maybe a month. The car wasn't the problem – it was the fact that I would abuse it so relentlessly.

I'd been working with Alfie since I'd moved down, which wasn't really working, to me it was just hanging out with a mate, who let me help him spend his money. But I needed to get a proper job now, which is when a cold, hard reality hit me. Without a single GCSE to my name, I would fall at the first hurdle. It would gradually dawn on me that dad's persistent enthusiasm behind "getting some grades" was far from a parent just "banging on". A result of having no qualifications was that, the only job I could get was in a warehouse, earning minimum wage, no prospects, no benefits just the same mind-numbing work, picking and packing orders every day for about £1000 a month, after tax and national insurance had been deducted, I be left with just over £800 – to last a whole month, I struggled to make that money last more than a week. This was where the penny well and truly dropped regarding qualifications. Just like always I still had, 'champagne taste,' I found this to be one of the most punishing parts of the lesson.

I'd made a couple of new mates working in the warehouse, one lad who was a year older than me, and his older brother. These boys would happily put in an 8-hour shift of this dull, tedious, monotonous work, which to me felt like banging my head against a brick wall, maybe not "happily" but they seemed much more content with the work-to-reward ratio. It was such a miserable, boring change from the excitement of drugs and guns – which oddly, I had begun to miss. These brothers were both big smokers and back then, most (if not all) evenings after work, they would just sit at home smoking. I joined in with this for a bit but would grow tired of this dramatic lifestyle change very soon.

Dad's encouraging words started ringing in my ears, "you get out of life, what you put in" considering this, I got another job as well as the warehouse work, delivering takeaways for a few hours each Friday and Saturday night for £50 a shift. Of course, at 17 years old I felt that my time was worth a bit more, I proposed "and a free meal at the end of each shift?" – the boss agreed. I was genuinely happy doing this, being paid to drive – not only was I accomplishing both of my top 'needs and wants' but, just like Alfie I was earning money from driving. This made my weekends "ok". I found the warehouse work torture, I stuck it out as long as I possibly could but, after about 6/7 months that was it.

I'll never forget when Alfie came to visit Dad's house once; I must have been about 13 at the time. He gave me a lift to school the following morning in the m3 he happened to be driving on this occasion. He took the much longer route and had the car properly sideways every chance he got. This was the sort of thing that crude dreams were made up of to a 13 -year-old boy, this cemented my desire to one day have my own BMW. Now 17, after hours and hours of research I found that, you couldn't get the insurance on a BMW, or in fact anything rear-wheel-drive - until you were at least 21 years old, nor could I find a way of making it "appear" legal. "Okay, well I just won't insure it then."

The next job I had was as a "drivers' mate" for one of Alfie's childhood friends – let's call him "Ricky". My time was divided between chain smoking his fags on long journeys, being "helpful" - strapping down, loading/unloading cargo at each end of the journey, and repairing wooden pallets, which was only slightly less monotonous than the warehouse work and for even less money, but preferable to that boring, tiresome, warehouse work.

Ricky's a good bloke, his unbelievably inappropriate humour, always thoroughly entertaining, which made long, boring trips easy, and he paid me cash, which was handy. I was only with Ricky for about 9 months, throughout that time I managed to fund the lifestyle of a 17-year-old, i.e. doing nothing in particular, abusing vehicles at every opportunity, and spending most of each weekend in one of the local public houses. With Ricky's help I managed to save up £800. I knew exactly what this was for, but I didn't tell anyone, as I knew full-well that this would never be legal – Anna-Marie was definitely going to moan at me.

I found this BMW in Essex, I decided that was the one I was going to buy, and I would tie this trip in with a visit up North, I've no idea why I didn't find one closer, I think I just fancied a bit of a trek. Anyway, I got the train there to go and view it, knowing full well that I'd buy it regardless of what I saw. It had no tax, no MOT, I didn't have any insurance but, none of that mattered to me, I was always going to have it. I drove it from Essex all the way up to Chester that evening; I was eager to show the boys.

To this day I still can't believe that I made it all the way from Essex to Chester in an untaxed, uninsured, unroadworthy car – without getting pulled. I arrived close to midnight. Even though I hadn't seen or spoken to these lads for the last year or so – nothing had changed. After chilling at Matt's house into the early hours, I was driving my girlfriend back to her house and I was planning to drop Jay off on the way, the journey had only just begun when blue lights appeared in my rear-view mirror. "Ahh…"

In my head the car would only be seized if it stopped on a public highway, but not if it was on private property (completely wrong by the way, as I would find out). I knew this area and route quite well, I had a mate that lived only a few miles away, my intention was to stop when I got onto his driveway so, I decided to put my foot down. Following some very desperate driving, I made it to this friend's house, and swung it in, old bill immediately behind me, ripping me out the car and taking me down hard, before jumping on top of me.

I was taken to the nearest available station, which on this occasion happened to be Mold, my most familiar station, I'd been coming here since before my teenage years. I was taken into the custody suite, as soon as I came into view of the counter I was recognised by the custody sergeant instantly, and there was a suited officer stood next to him, who dropped his head into his hands upon seeing me, I heard, "Ooh, Greg!" – he'd always been a uniformed PC, every time he'd arrested me; he now wore a suit. Our catch up was limited, he then let the CS take over.

I was charged and bailed, Alfie came all the way up North; to collect me and the BMW and we drove back to Somerset.

It was about 6 weeks before I would have to go back up North for the court case, Alfie did the driving. My solicitor had advised me to "prepare for the worst" - I was thinking "this is it".

On the way there, we called into a café just before arriving, the atmosphere between us felt tense, 'was this going to be my last meal before jail?' When entering the court building, a group who were familiar with someone I owed money too, spotted me and started talking amongst themselves, I started thinking the worst – but "whatever" my mind was too busy thinking about the case.

Despite the driving ban that had been added to my record just over a year ago, I got away with; the maximum length ban for the offense, of three years and a couple more conviction codes were added to my license – ha, I couldn't believe it.

Down south, Winscombe, where I lived was just outside of Cheddar, which was the areas hub, in terms of stuff happening, socialising etc. Around Cheddar and its surrounding areas there were barely any police. There was a police station in Cheddar, you would notice their vehicle had moved now and then but, apart from that you wouldn't ever see "police activity". So, I didn't ever completely stop driving. Everyone knew I was banned; the family who were aware didn't approve of it but, knew that they couldn't stop me. I was of adult age now and I wouldn't have taken any notice of whoever tried giving me any sort of "be careful" speech, I was going to do exactly what I wanted.

Around this time, I found a better suited group of mates. No one in this group was a stranger to the law. These lads were much more like-minded, nothing remotely close to the kind of antics I'd been involved in up North, this bunch were more into drinking, socialising and the occasional altercation here and there, and there, oh and over there too. "Yeah, these boys enjoyed a good punch-up."

Living down south, not much changed with regards to always being skint, due to my tragic financial circumstances I started looking for work again, yes obviously I had the same problem as before – "no GCSE's blah blah blah", and now on top of that no driving license, living in such a rural location exaggerated this problem.

'San' my brothers mum, spotted a job for me in the local paper. I looked into it, "trainee bathroom fitter, 8-4 Monday to Friday" perfect, not only didn't it mention anything about qualifications but, the guy actually lived in the street behind my house, I called and was invited round for an interview. Walking between our front doors took no more than 3 minutes, so, getting to work wouldn't ever be a problem. I became an assistant bathroom fitter. I worked alongside the boss, of the company, I found him to be nothing less than a truly dedicated, perfectionist. I found the work physically demanding which I enjoyed. Over the next year or so, I unintentionally picked up on just how much of a physical toll it was taking on my boss. He was middle aged, an avid cyclist, went to the gym 5 nights a week, didn't drink, didn't smoke, he was in really good shape. But his knees and back were suffering, along with most of his other bones judging by the horrific cracks and clicks I heard throughout the day. After understanding this issue, a nagging thought started developing, "I don't want to be in that kind of shape at that age, (oh the irony) I can do better than this. I don't have any GCSEs, but I've got a decent head on my shoulders, I think? I wish I could go to college; I want to follow in my dad's footsteps, I want to go to work wearing a suit". After months of tormenting myself with thoughts like these, I decided to run it by my boss, he laughed this "silly idea" off, as did the others I ran the idea by. To be fair from what "others" knew of me, I wasn't even anywhere near the same universe – in terms of being/becoming student material.

Around this time the UK went into recession, my boss mentioned that "keeping me full time was becoming difficult". This marked the end of the full-time bathroom fitting work. This meant I had a tremendous amount more free time, which ultimately just meant loads more time for the above thoughts to stew.

"You get out of life, what you put in", these words were on repeat, bouncing round my head 24/7. Eventually, I thought "right that's it, I'm going for it". Now 18 years old, this would be where I started to build my future. I was confident I had the ability, and now I had the drive.

Excited by the idea, as soon as I got the chance, I wanted to "get the ball rolling". I had half a day's work with my bathroom guy coming up in Weston-Super-Mare, "perfect, I'll do the first half of the day with him, then get the train to Bridgewater" (the location of the closest, reputable college). 18 years old, I went into Bridgewater College to find out about getting onto a course that would get me qualified in "something businessy". I met with one of the main lecturers in control of the admissions. I'd done a messy morning's work ripping out an old bathroom, and my appearance matched. I told this lady I wanted a place on the "Business Studies" course, this lecturer obviously judged this book by its cover, and clearly thought I was in the wrong place, she double checked that I knew I was in "the business block", eventually she agreed to talk with me. We took a seat, she began by asking me a few questions, GCSE's, education, work experience etc, the answer to every single question did nothing but reinforce her hesitation. It felt like she started trying to sort of put me off the idea, by emphasising the demanding academic input required, the continuously testing work, and the fact that "even some of the most qualified students on the course have trouble, and around a third of students on this course don't see it through". By this point, her intentions felt obvious, I could have taken the hint, but I continued to counter her answers. Eventually I'd kept-on long enough to discover that, sitting 2 years of "key studies" would cater for my lack of GCSE's and providing I achieved the required grades, I could then go on to sit the 2-year business studies course. "So, I won't qualify for four years? That's a lot longer than I was hoping but, what needs must".

I continued with questions, "Surely there's a quicker way?" Then in the most mature, responsible, eloquent voice I could manage, as delicately as possible I said, "don't let the fact that I didn't manage to get any GCSE's, help you make your decision, I am perfectly capable in terms of my key studies". I then gave her some BS that "I didn't sit the exams because I was moving house" or something like that.

I kept on enough for her to mention that, sitting and passing an "entrants' exam" would be enough to cut out the 2 years of "key studies". I immediately put myself forward for that, claiming "that wouldn't be a problem". This wasn't of any concern, I thought, I'd have at least a few days to prepare myself, which I felt I would need, at that point I felt completely alien to anything academic. She carried on talking, I kind of zoned out – daydreaming about the idea of turning my ambition into reality. With 1 ear on what she was saying, I heard enough to understand that I was expected to sit the exam in the building next door in the next 30 minutes. "Oh shid!" Well, I can't back out now, especially after giving it all that "yea sure – I'm perfectly capable."

So, I went to sit the exam, obviously I felt nervous but, more than that, it felt so good to be in an academic environment again, the questions on the screen in front of me had me using parts of my brain that hadn't been used for what felt like so long, I remember really enjoying the experience. Soon enough, I'd reached the end of the test, there was parts I struggled on but overall, I really enjoyed it, and I was confident that I'd done ok.

I made my way back over to see the lecturer concerned, I didn't know this at the time, but she already had my results. She was in the staff's office, she knew that I was there, so I just waited outside the office, she was taking ages, my mind was racing, "what's she doing?" "Maybe, I was overconfident?" "Maybe she's discussing my case with her seniors?" "Maybe there's some technicality that means I won't be allowed on the course?"

Eventually, she came out with an odd look on her face and said, "Well done Mr Sumner, you've got a place on the course, see you in

September." The tone in which she said this explained that look on her face, she was clearly a bit sort of taken back, I think she may have felt a tad guilty for judging me? Anyway, I felt great! That day felt like an enormous stride towards my vision of becoming "something".

Armed with this new opportunity, the day-to-day incessant, screaming concern, regarding my future having absolutely zero prospects, quietened to background noise. The frequency and nature of interactions with the same group of friends carried on just like normal, so that meant the same old antics, nights jam-packed full of questionable behaviour, with a mild-moderate peppering of illegal stuff. Nights out normally always included finding/provoking a fight in whichever area we happened to be in, meaning yes, in the gap between gaining a place on the course and the academic year starting, I did get into a spot of bother with the law, once or twice.

In the years before this point, I had been constantly getting into trouble for general nuisance stuff, I was on "pub watch" throughout the area, I had been almost since first moving down. I was well known locally, always for the wrong reasons – that kind of yob. The courts were running out of options. I can't remember what for exactly, but they gave me a hefty sentence of community service to 'wake me up'. I had absolutely zero intension of ever doing any community service, I didn't even go to the induction, back to court - where sharing information on my college admission held tremendous weight, they decided "instead of community service, we're giving you the equivalent of double the sentence of "house arrest" (police tag). I was only allowed out from 7a.m. to 6p.m. I was clearly told "the alternative is prison Mr. Sumner, this is your last chance". After hearing this, I sincerely vowed never ever to get into trouble again, "Hmmm, that sounds familiar…"

It was now September I was 19, and it was the first day of my course. I was only about 12months into my 3-year driving ban when starting, so I had to get the college bus, a service that only ran each way once a day. There I was, at the bus stop first thing, raring to go, excited about being back in education. I was so eager to prove that there was more to Greg than what I had shown. Cheddar to Bridgwater on the college's bus, was an awkward journey across the moors, public transport wasn't an option, I needed to be at the bus stop for 8am Mon-Friday. It felt like the journey took forever, but I didn't care - I couldn't wait to get stuck in.

For the first few months of college, I was living with a couple I'd known for years, friends of my brother. They knew I was looking for somewhere to live and kindly offered me their spare room rent free. Their place was overlooking the road running between 2 of the busiest pubs in the village, it couldn't have been any more central. I found it impossible to stick to the curfew

When I started at college, I was eager to get a girlfriend. Baring this in mind, I'd made friends with a girl called Sophie who also lived in Cheddar, she got the same bus to college. She already had a boyfriend so, unfortunately for her I slipped through her fingers. On weekends, I would often go round to her house to chill, one day a friend of hers called Abi was there. Apart from her name, everything about her was flawless, the closest I'd ever seen to a physical 10 but, when I tried hitting on her she wasn't having any of it. She had a boyfriend, she proved her loyalty, I could see that this wasn't the right time, I would certainly find her for a "catch up" in the future.
One night around this time, I was out just having a quiet drink with a couple of mates, it was the weekend - so was outside of my curfew-hours of course. There was an irregular amount of people out in the village because of the "Beach Race", a motorbike race held annually in Weston-Super-Mare. Me and 2 friends were walking through

Cheddar, from one pub to the next and there happened to be 3 men walking towards us, no doubt doing the same as we were in reverse order. Moments after passing us, they started making snide comments, at such a volume so as making it clear that they were intending to be heard.

These poor blokes were obviously out on the lash whilst away from home, and just fancied a bit of a ruckus after a few drinks. I knew that feeling all too well, as did the other lads present. We turned just enough to glance over our shoulders, to see what all the fuss was about, and found they had stopped walking, turned to face us, and were pointing at us and saying provocative stuff, clearly a confrontation?

Once their intentions were clear we all ran at each other and had a brief "disagreement" right there in the street. These guys must have been well and truly pooped because, before you know it, they all decided to have a nap right there, in the middle of the road.

With the influx of people in the village, there was also an influx of police, unluckily for us the police just happened to be passing, each of us darted off in different directions, they soon found and arrested me and 1 other.

They took us to Bridgewater police station, following the standard night's sleep on those useless mattresses, I/we were charged and released; CPS (Crown Prosecution Service), soon got it touch, I was heading back to court.
It was the morning of my court case, we'd been on a bit of a knees-up, for a few days/nights, as a last send-off sort of thing. A friend was taking me there, on the way, we stopped off at a mate's house to see his new "crosser" (off-road motorbike).
"Give it here" I said, like an absolute moron - considering that I hadn't slept for over 48hours. I got on the bike, it was only a little 80cc, 2-

stroke thing, but the acceleration was immense. I discovered this as the front wheel took to the air halfway round a sweeping bend, meaning I had no control of the steering, I crashed through/over someone's front garden fence and landed on/in their paved garden, hard. The bike was a mess and so was my left knee, it ballooned instantly, judging by friend's reactions - it looked bad. Being so heavily self-medicated, I couldn't feel it, so it was of no concern to me at the time. We were on our way to court, so I was helped back into the car, and we carried on.

When summoned to magistrate's court, no individual times are given, everyone is given either a morning or an afternoon slot and you must sit and wait in the same room, until you get called in. My mate practically carried me into the court building. I was wearing shorts. Whilst entering, I could see that others in the waiting room were horrified by the sight of my knee, asking if I was okay, offering me their seats, showing real concern.

I don't know the story I gave – or if anyone even asked, but my case was rushed through. I remember being commended, they were so impressed that I'd "prioritised court, managing to make it despite suffering an injury of such significance". Such selflessness bought considerable brownie points with the magistrates, enough so as to escape a custodial. They just added some more time to my police tag and warned me to take the curfew more seriously.

Shortly after recovering from the above, I was up in court again for ignoring my curfew "blah-blah-blah", I'd ripped it off this time – and gone out on the lash. Upon entering the courthouse, I bumped into a friend of mine Alex, he was there supporting another mate. Whilst being sat there for hours he came up with a new blag - I should blame being useless with the curfew on "problematic living arrangements", then propose just finding somewhere else to live – problem solved. Alex had said I could move in at his, I just needed the court to recognise the problem and agree with this solution – they did, great "cheers Al!". Alex still lived at home with his family. A solid, structured, family environment perfect, this was exactly what I needed. This change helped me to live a much more structured, disciplined lifestyle. Everyone in the house was either working or in full time education, I would finally respect the boundaries of my ankle bracelet. A tremendous thanks to, Jill, Rex, and Alex.

As a result, I was now much more committed to college, I gave up smoking, drinking, unnecessary socialising, ensuring I dedicated myself entirely to the course. Despite now sleeping on Al's bedroom floor, I managed to stay focused by picturing the end-goal, me suited and booted looking ridiculously suave, and of course a legal BMW was never too far from my thoughts. For the first time, I stuck to my curfew.

Since the start of my course, my greatest concern was my tag being seen. This was easy to conceal but on the occasion another student spotted it I'd make up something ridiculous like; "I got caught speeding on my pushbike", I was "new Greg" now, I wanted to be known for different reasons, my brother is so widely known simply for being such a decent bloke, "I can do that".

After a couple of months, fellow students were aware that I was wearing a tag and that I was a few years older. Naturally, there was a lot of curiosity. As I didn't know anyone on the course, I think others were sceptical of me to begin with but, it didn't take long for my adorable personality to come beaming through. After this becoming apparent, I found it felt noticeably different, to be known solely for being "a decent bloke".

The tag was now common knowledge amongst my class. Making other students laugh with the excuses I gave, always provoked more questions. When I felt the time had come, I broke it too Alan - my tutor, that I was wearing a police tag, along with a very light explanation as to why, he looked towards me, paused (clearly having a good think, my heart's racing, I'm panicking by this point) he takes a deep breath in, before saying "S'alright, that was then, this is now, as far as I'm concerned the fact that your here, and eager to get your BTEC speaks for itself". This was a big relief – his response was reassuring.

Academically I was able to manage somewhat easily, I already had a basic idea of a lot of the topics. Over the years, Dad had been continuously drip-feeding me little bits of information/advice here and there.

I remember there was one lesson, the teacher was going over something. Rather than paying attention I was on my phone or fiddling, something like that. She turned to me and said, "right Greg, what do you think would happen in that scenario?", intending to catch me out. Everyone, including the teacher was well aware that I hadn't been paying any attention whatsoever, but I just blurted out a load of business sounding jargon, she looked at me – rather shocked, "yes, yes, absolutely. Good point, well done." – yeah, I was that sort of tinker/twot.

My end goal was to simply get that piece of paper that an employer would see and could tick the relevant box. I wasn't aiming for a mind-blowing distinction – all's I needed was a pass, enough to simply get my foot in the door. I did get some support from the government in terms of receiving money to live, paying rent etc, which was helpful, the college helped too. Student Union set me up with a food card, providing me with £30 credit each week to use in the canteen. I realised that if you want to get on and educate or better yourself there is plenty of support available. So don't ever be afraid to approach the relevant person, people, authority, "If you don't ask – you don't get."

Whilst I was living with Alex's family, I had my feet firmly on the ground, I did not breach my tag once. As the busses only ran at the beginning and end of the day, regardless of what time my lessons were, I would spend the whole day at college. By the time I got home I only had an hour and a half before my curfew. Alex was a gym freak, so I started going to the gym with him. Before long I was hooked, Alex set a decent little routine. I would get back from college, get changed and go straight to the gym for an hour, then by the time I'd walked back home there would only be a few minutes left before 6pm, by this time Jill would've gotten home and made dinner, perfect. I felt every available minute of my day was being utilised. I'd always had absolutely zero interest in even considering the idea of going to a gym – "it's hard to improve on perfection." But, having something reliably repetitive to occupy my time and plug the measly gap between college and my curfew fitted in just rite. I'd go 6 days a week (they'd be closed Sundays) and would pump out a reasonable session every time. I even went as far as starting to monitor my diet, trying to ensure I was eating the right foods. With Alex training me, my stable, structured lifestyle and Jill's hearty, healthy, home cooked meals, I was soon in decent shape, in my opinion anyway, a clear change from the bag of bones that I had always been.

Whilst "getting my feet on the ground" at Alex's, I wanted to get a job. I understood that Alex's mum always had "an ear to the ground" considering stuff going on locally, I asked Jill for help finding a job, she put me in touch with a local businessman called Julian, he had a couple of businesses in the village at the time. Not only did he give me some paid work that was relevant to my BTEC, but he would also take me with him up to Bristol once a week, to his early morning networking meetings. Jules would get me to stand up and talk in front of the room full of professionals. I've never had any trouble "giving the big I am" in front of whoever but, doing this – my heart was in my mouth, I'd always been a very forward lad socially, but something like this needed a different kind of confidence. I never ever enjoyed doing this but, after reminding myself about "taking the rough with the smooth" I would push myself into doing it - Thank you Jules mate – always were and still are a massive help.

I lived with Alex and his family until about halfway through my first year of college. After completing the sentence of house arrest, it took about 6 weeks and then I got a one-bedroom flat closer to the centre of Cheddar. The novelty of my new living arrangements got the better of me and I got carried away living the life of a young, single student. It was the first time I had ever lived completely on my own and I found staying focused on my studies impossibly difficult. I had lost the stabilising influence of living with a family, and the sense of discipline that came with it, which meant I never said no to any offer of "socialising." A consequence of this was that my attendance dropped at college. To lessen the impact on getting my BTEC. I always made sure that I kept track of where they were up to on the course, by checking in with Alan, via email.

I probably attended college about 60% of the time, whenever offered a day's work, I would take it, but the main reason would usually be to recover from the night before. I found that if I missed a day, a week, or even the best part of a month, I found it easy to catch up.

Realising how much my lifestyle was impacting on my studies, when that tenancy came to an end, I knew I had to pay some attention to this. I moved to Worle on the edge of Weston-Super-Mare, I chose this location as it was far away enough from town to be a problematic commute – so I wouldn't be 'out' every night, and it was just 'round the corner' from a train platform, which was on a direct route to Bridgewater. Train travel being an option, added much greater flexibility. My attendance shot up as a result. It was a much nicer place but paying the rent was always difficult, "Champagne taste, lemonade pockets" ever since I was young. Paying rent was always last on my list of priorities and meant cycling round to the landlord's house to drop off a handful of borrowed cash more than once.

Around the end of the previous tenancy I'd acquired a girlfriend, she was perfect all round, a little bit older, had a degree, a good job, nice car, and she was mature – not in a boring way but, in a helpful, constructive, reliable, dependable way, at that age, this was "my type" exactly, she pretty much lived with me – having her stabilising influence round, helped so much.
One night after my 20th birthday, I went to go raise a glass with some friends, as the evening was coming to an end, I'd somehow gotten the attention of a pretty blonde, I already kind of knew her, we had some mutual friends, and I often saw her around town, so she was a familiar face. She lived near town, when the time came, I walked her home and ended up joining her for another drink.
A short time later I received a call from the above, telling me she was pregnant. I couldn't believe it, I was instantly brimmed with excitement, joy, happiness. I felt so lucky, I'd been anxiously awaiting having kids of my own for so long.
One evening I invited her round to my place so we could talk. While we were chatting, I planted the seed of naming the baby "Alfie", if the baby were to be a boy - she liked the name too. But conversation moved on quickly as there was so much more to discuss.

The idea of being a constructive, supportive, and reliable parent, was just ridiculous, I could barely look after myself. I had a fair bit of growing up to do before being competent of fatherhood. I didn't even have a job, income, or stable home, I was a student, living off the state.

It's not that I doubted Alfie's mother in any way but, the thought of a DNA test seemed like an appropriate step for someone in my position? They were a few hundred quid then, on top of affording to live, this was an unattainable cost to me at the time.

For the first few months, I stopped by every single chance I got but then, something changed, something unseen and unheard, had become involved and was not willing to let this continue. I still did whatever possible to see baby Alf, I somehow managed to find out that Alfie's auntie had him 1 day a week whilst his mum worked, I got in touch and arranged to go and spend some time with baby Alf, sadly this opportunity never occurred again. Long before I had reached the end of my BTEC, a gap both physical and circumstantial had developed between me and Alfie's mother, we both had partners, and I had to move back to Cheddar, not at all to avoid the situation. But because, I was no longer a student, the government took a step back in terms of helping financially, meaning I simply couldn't afford to live on my own. I needed a roof over my head, and this was where the home of my girlfriend was, she'd invited me to go and live with her in her family's home back in Cheddar. Initially for just a couple of weeks, as some things do in life, those weeks turned into months.

By this point, 'rumours' were flying round about me having a baby, it seemed to be common knowledge. Whilst at the girlfriends one evening, her dad came into the room and asked me to step outside with him, he told me he had heard that I have fathered a child. I told him it was just malicious gossip and there was no truth in it, my skin started crawling before I even finished the sentence, I've told an array of lies to a wide range of people over the years, but a lie of this nature felt so much worse, I hated myself for it but, still needed a roof over my head.

The combination of the above mixed with my personal life turning chaotic again, were majorly damaging factors. It had now been quite some time between this point and when I last saw Alfie. It was approaching his 1st birthday, I didn't have a penny to my name but, I ensured that a handful of carefully thought-out, meaningful gifts made it to Alf for his birthday. I'm very ashamed to admit, I wasn't around for Alfie's first year. I watched from a distance (social media), from everything I saw, the man there instead of me was clearly fulfilling the father role, I would have done more harm than good if I'd have involved Alfie in my turbulent, unstable life. By no means can I ever justify the way I allowed the situation to develop, I know I dealt with the matter terribly, nothing could ever make up for that period, I will never forgive myself.

Chapter 6

After college

2011

"The devil finds work for idle hands..."

At the end of the course, most of the others were taking some time out – a gap year. After setting up a couple of interviews and being accepted by one of them, I had the choice of either going to university "Greg Sumner - University whaaaat!" or getting a job. The DNA was my most urgent priority so after finally becoming a possibility, for the first time in my life I wanted to establish a reliable income and start chipping away at my debt, enabling me to afford a test as soon as possible.

Despite my character, lifestyle, experiences, history, habits, people I associated with and my considerably lengthy list of criminal convictions, I have always interviewed well. Because I could easily portray myself as an upstanding citizen. I would just think to myself – "what would Dad expect?". Baring this in mind I had a pretty good idea of what to do, say, at what point and the best way to say it, how to introduce and hold myself etc. They would have absolutely no reason to suspect me of being anything other than how I presented. I've always found it easy to present myself well, Dad had effortlessly, sub-consciously demonstrated a masterclass in the above, throughout my childhood. Personal presentation is everything, this generates positivity which, projects confidence, I believe and have always told myself that confidence, breeds success. Out of every single job interview I've ever sat, each has asked about a criminal record but, not one ever felt it necessary to do a background check. Obviously, the question always comes up and when it did, I'd sort of smirk and say, "me?" as if a completely outrageous idea.

While on the BTEC course, Alex's mum told me that, she knew where there would be a job for me after I qualified. Jill stayed true to her word and got me an interview. It came as no surprise to me at all, the owner was so content with me and my character – he offered me the job there and then, in the initial interview.

The job was in sales, so this was right up my street. The company was owned and run by a father and his two sons. I was only 20, straight out of college and straight into an £18k a year job (an immense starting wage in 2011). This was quite a bit more money than any previous job I'd had, ever paid me.

The company had two departments. One was the biggest hospital supplier in the U.K, of the device to help with intubation. The other sold second-hand hospital equipment, "sounds ropey, I know, I thought the same until I found out that vets' practices were always the buyers of this stuff." One son did the new medical equipment, the other took care of the second-hand stuff, with the father overseeing everything.

The starting salary was beyond belief, it should have been a dream job. In the first couple of months, I had managed to get a little studio flat in Cheddar, it was a bit of a shack, the heating/hot water and electric were all incredibly temperamental but, at £300pcm, bills included, this was what I could afford.

The owner and both sons all had very nice German cars, at the beginning the thought of getting something similar helped me dedicate 110% of my, will, passion, interest, energy, my entire being went into learning the role. My driving ban came to an end shortly after starting here, within a couple of months, and with the help of my girlfriend, I managed to get a legal BMW, my own little 3-series! I took this off a friend's hands, along with the debt left on the vehicle. "I know, I know not a very smart move but, I was young and excited", besides there was no way I'd have been able to save for a car, so I took it on with its debt. It may have been nine years old, but it was the newest car I'd ever owned. "I'd actually done it", my aspirations were beginning to materialise. For the first time in my life everything seemed to be falling into place, I could feel sorting the paternity dilemma getting closer.

They sent me on a night course to learn about web design, even though I completed the course, I never got the chance to put my newly learnt skills into practice. Next, they sent me with one of the sons up to an exhibition in Edinburgh, we flew up there then drove a rather plush hire car from Edinburgh airport over to Glasgow University where we spent a day doing a course on something relevant, before returning across to Edinburgh, where we spent the night, before presenting at a show the following day.

I couldn't believe I was being paid to fly up country, stay in a very nice hotel, with all costs covered throughout the trip. I thought 'this is the life'. I had heard dad talk of his employers going to this extent enough times, this emphasised my feeling of achievement. Being mindful not to seem like I was expecting, when looking for somewhere to go for dinner that evening, I was looking for somewhere reasonable in terms of price. We passed a few of the usual well-known high-street restaurants, I suggested more than 1 of those but, the boss's son wasn't up for that, he had spotted a fine steakhouse smack bang, in the middle of the Highstreet, with a perfect view of Edinburgh Castle. I sat there enjoying my expensive steak dinner with all the trimmings, courtesy of the company, "I could get used to this!" This whole excursion resulted in an overwhelming sense of personal accomplishment, which was new? My urge to get on with succeeding was at its most potent. 'Right, what's next!'

Back in the office, there were just the four of us (the owner, both sons and I) occupying the vast mezzanine level of the office space.

I was more than eager to prove myself, learn more, experience more, become a worthy, valued member of the team and actually be relied on for something, I was hungry to get stuck into an active role, I wanted to do well with and for this company. I had big plans for my role here. The process of getting me out "into the field" was slow, practically stationery, literally non-existent. Whilst in the office I spent 95% of my time researching the company's stock list, which was sizable, to say the least. The boss would hand me a copy of their catalogue and say, "Here you are, you can read up on some of our products." Apart from a brief description and a product code, I wasn't learning anything about the item, when selling anything - knowledge is power, especially when selling something you know nothing about, to someone who does know and has experience with.

Despite the above, I just knuckled down and did the best I could, of getting to know the products, I would research what they did and how they worked online. These three men were not sporty types, I was close to being in the best shape of my life, I was twenty-one years old, bursting full of energy, raring to get out on the road and start selling, a young man in a hurry to accomplish whatever task presented itself. I understood that I needed to know what I was selling but at the same time I wanted to scream "I'm here, I'm qualified, I'm willing, I'm waiting, I want to sell – please get me in front of someone!"

Any progression in my role here felt entirely fictitious. The thought of achieving any of my goals here started to dwindle, because of this I got bored with the job, after months of sitting in the silent office for 8 hours a day, my dream of doing well here never stopped fading and soon ran out altogether, this impacted on my enthusiasm. One day whilst talking with the oldest son, one of the questions he asked was "How much are we paying you?" – as he was my senior, I just answered him honestly.

Shortly after, he started saying things like "Are you happy here?" "Don't you get bored here sometimes?" "What is your dream job?" Since I told him my salary, I got nothing but a very clear feeling of uneasiness regarding my employment, it became apparent that there wasn't any chance of a future at this place. After a week or so, of this nature of conversation, he mentioned that they could let me go with about three grand in my pocket, I'd had enough, I took it.

All that money went towards debts so, there I was again, empty pockets, struggling to afford to live, absolutely nothing regarding any job prospects, I was very familiar with these exact circumstances, along with this feeling of hopelessness that always accompanies such headspace.

Since my teenage years, crime/criminals were never far away, very much a standard daily interaction, I had built decent friendships with these people over the years, these were my friends, and the people I spent most of my time with. During the period following becoming unemployed again, I started hanging out with someone new, this lad was notorious, I don't mean a bit of a nuisance, I mean seriously bad. Not even the areas well-known, rowdiest of the older lot were willing to confront this lad, regardless of however they might have been involved personally, everyone was mindful of not upsetting him. He was not even popular amongst the "bad lads", he was a different breed of bad. He wasn't visually intimidating in the slightest – far from it, he just didn't care, and he was also close with a group of even more dangerous and criminally willing individuals known nationally. To top it off - fire was of no concern, I'll say no more.

Not someone I'd ever hung around with or even met before, I'd just heard his name mentioned in some unimaginable rumours. I don't remember how our paths crossed but, we started hanging around together, we were both skint, so we'd devote most of our time and attention to finding ways to make money. About 2 months passed and, in that time, I got arrested 2 or 3 times, my list of charges ranged from burglary to possession of a firearm, and my flat got raided too, years of "souvenirs" got confiscated/reclaimed.

I'm not going to say who from but, we'd been told about a brand-new Land Rover, and keys that could be "easily accessed".

Through a friend of a friend, I had pre-arranged the sale, with a group in Devon. Before we took the vehicle, we worked out a plan, how to get onto the premises, getting the keys, locating the vehicle, the best route, then where to meet.
When it was dark, we went to the area concerned in my car, I parked and left the friend with my motor – his job was to take my car to the rendezvous point.
After looking enthusiastically/raiding the relevant areas, I found the keys, then located the vehicle, hopped in and drove away following the agreed route. We met up again, before proceeding onto the next point – meeting the buyers at the pre-arranged location.
The journey took about an hour, we parked the Defender up and went to a nearby pub, where I had some dinner, while we waited. Anxious to get things underway that evening, we'd arrived quite some

time before planned, we got bored of waiting and decided to head home and return to complete the transaction the following day.
I was driving perfectly fine, keeping to the speed limit etc. But I accidentally ran a red light and ironically there was a police car right behind us. Blue lights started flashing and we were pulled over. Naturally, whenever I've encountered the police, when something illegal has happened or is happening, my mind goes into overdrive anticipating police's questions, then inventing scenarios and excuses, making them watertight, relevant and hopefully therefore believable. Worryingly, for the 1st time ever, that sort of helpful, constructive panic didn't occur. I could see the keys to the Land Rover we'd just taken, in my passenger footwell - at my mates' feet. I knew this was going to be trouble, I just don't think I could be bothered to care? The copper came over armed with his torch and little handheld device, at first it was just like every other time I had been pulled over. License, tax, insurance, along with the condition of my tires and vehicle in general. I was breathalysed - I was not over the limit; I'd barely touched the pint I ordered with my food. I explained "Sorry, I'm not from the area and simply didn't see the red light". The copper said "yeah, don't worry – that's a common problem at these particular lights" things were looking good, and we were all set to continue our journey.

Then we were both asked to "exit the vehicle please" - 'here we go'. They found the Land Rover keys in the passenger footwell straight away. When asked about the keys my mate obviously didn't want to admit to anything, neither did I, we both kept quiet, so they picked up that something was fishy. I did consider interjecting, but through experience I have found that when a copper has a hunch, any interjection normally just prolongs the outcome, particularly when there is physical evidence to explain/debate.

They started searching the car more closely. One of them pulled out a black case from the glovebox. He put it on the roof of the car, opened it, and pulled out a taser.

"Oh yeah…"

It's gonna be a loonng night.

I had been given the taser by someone who owed me some money a few days previous. I'd never used it, nor did I ever intend to. It was just an interesting item to possess.
We were both handcuffed and taken to Exeter police station. We got checked into the station, allocated a cell, fingerprinted, DNA swabbed, and I was strip searched, before being put in my cell.
Then, when the time comes to be interviewed, you are assigned a duty solicitor if you agree to having one. I don't always but I did this time, I had the feeling this was going to be trouble, so felt I needed all the help I could get. When mine finally rocked up, I immediately noticed just how scruffy he was, if that guy was claiming to be a legally qualified professional, I shouldn't have been the only one cuffed up. I kid you not, the man had a piece of bailer twine round his waist, in place of a belt.
Anyway, you can't choose so, I had no choice but to have this guy. He was of no help whatsoever, the interview was just him reiterating the severity of the charges, along with potential sentences "this kind of taser is a firearm under section 5 of the UK's firearms act. So, possessing one is a very serious offence, you'll be looking at…". My mind was boiling over, 'who the fluk is this guy? What is he playing at?' I have met many duty solicitors over the years, so I have a good enough understanding of their role throughout this process and this guy was not even close to fulfilling the supposed role. I began to

panic, it honestly felt like he was just one of their (the coppers') mates, playing the role of a solicitor for entertainment. In an attempt to get him to engage more effectively I started dropping crumbs, hinting to the guy that my dad had a big firm of solicitors up North, hoping he might have thought that I could be a worthy person to know (Yes, I know, but I really was clutching at straws). During the time between being arrested and getting through the interview with this clown, the police had sussed the scenario, those keys, stolen Landy nearby etc, not only had the severity of the charges and potential sentence worsened but the reality of trouble really had dawned on me. We left the station the following day with some hefty charges. The weapon possession was the most severe, and all their evidence regarding 'acquiring' the Land Rover and the route we took was unbelievably accurate. Thanks to GPRS, and ANPR, they had tracked each of the vehicles for 96% of the journey. Forgetting to take the above into account was truly a schoolboy error, I vaguely recall almost being caught out by GPRS before, I can't believe it never even crossed my mind – goes to show just how out of touch with criminality I'd become by this point.

I didn't know then and I wouldn't say even if I did know now, but I'm still completely unaware of exactly what was said/agreed between those involved. But long story short I walked out of Taunton Crown Court with a 4-year sentence, suspended for 2 years! An astonishingly light slap on the wrist.

Chapter 7

In my element

Mid-2012

The tenancy at the studio flat in Cheddar was coming to an end and, perhaps not surprisingly, the owners didn't let Greg Sumner renew his tenancy, after that police raid, they had woken to the fact that I wasn't a saint.

I moved in with the family of an old friend of my brothers. This friend was working in the nearby Hilton Hotel at the time, one of those grand countryside Hiltons. She had been working at that hotel for years already.

She didn't always stay at the family home; as would often be working away. On one of the occasions our paths crossed, and we had time to talk, during our mostly aimless chit-chat, I gathered that the health club at the hotel was looking for a salesman. She hesitantly pointed me in the right direction, hesitantly as she had known me personally since I'd moved down here, she knew me – right down to the real nitty-gritty. This was a gamble on her behalf; to lesson her involvement, she did nothing more than mention the vacancy - I applied, my application was shortlisted, and I was called in for an interview, "that's all's I need, just show me the door and you'll see me dance through it! Watch this…"

In preparation for the interview, I ensured that I was well rested both physically and mentally. After a few tweaks here 'n' there I knew I would look positively breath-taking. I'd been finely groomed, beard, hair, skin, everything right down to my eyebrows. Attention to detail is key, especially when making first impressions, presentation says a lot about you but always comes second to punctuality, being punctual is critical and confidence always helps too – there is a fine line between confidence and arrogance, being mindful of this is essential.

There was no shadow of a doubt in my mind that I was the best candidate for the job by a country mile. I felt great driving there in my BMW dressed to the nines, designer suit, shirt, shoes, tie, belt everything right down to my socks, I'd paid attention to every little detail even selecting the most appropriate of my aftershaves. On that day, I was back in my upcoming businessman head. They would've been crazy not to have given me the job. There were three or four other candidates, they had dressed to impress too but I was in a different league, "that's what I was telling myself anyway". The interview was being held by a panel, made up of the health Club's manager and the managers of each department, Sales, Spa, Gym, and the Restaurant's Manager.

I felt nervous, I hadn't ever done one of these outside of a room full of friends in college, nah it wouldn't have been nervous nerves - I would have just been anxious to present this lucky team with the opportunity of employing me, Greg Sumner – salesman extraordinaire. (I believed that) I had learnt and mastered over the years how to present nerves as confidence, I thrive under pressure, especially in front of a crowd. I had spent a couple of nights preparing and rehearsing my presentation.
"I am DEFINITELY going to get this job; I WILL become a valuable part of this workforce."
I'd convinced myself; I was sure of it. I have proven to myself many times throughout my life that positive outcomes normally always follow a reassuring dose of self-belief; this inspires optimism, resulting in confidence.

When it came to my turn to present, I was ready, whoever was about to see my presentation – was about to be blown away, whoever was about to interview me would leave the room afterwards mind-blown, completely lost, as to how on earth they'd ever managed without me. I was slick, well prepared and ready.

For me, light humour has always been my favourite and most effective way to gauge an audience, and I believe effectively shows confidence, 'use humour to project confidence – what me? Pfft... I could write a book on that'. Dad could compose an encyclopaedia on people skills, wit and charm, and it had rubbed off on me... 'I kept telling myself'.

I was using my laptop that I got during my studies, tucked in the side of it was a remote, to control PowerPoint. I hadn't ever used it before; at the beginning of my presentation, I pulled it out with a bit of a flourish and said with the straightest, most sincere face, "Right so - this remote... I've never used it before, if this works successfully then I will take full credit for it, if not – it's the computers fault entirely and shouldn't reflect on me in any way, shape or form." It got the room chuckling, this felt good. I was completely free of any angst, worry, doubt, nerves – I was about to make this mine for sure.

I knew the job was right for me. I was a gym enthusiast, their facilities along with every piece of equipment within, was all amazing stuff, absolutely no expense spared, I knew I could successfully pitch one of these high-end memberships to anyone. An effective pitch is much easier when you know and believe in your product.

Inevitably, I got the job, I would start at the bottom on 16 grand a year, but I was delighted.

> "Show me the ladder and watch me climb"

I had used quite a few different gyms of varying qualities over the years, enough to be able to see this gym, was 10/10. As well as having all the best equipment it was obvious that no corners had been cut - every inch of the place was immaculate, the members even matched the facility. I already knew the market and I admired what I was selling so it felt like a perfect match. I wasn't earning as much as at my last job yet, but it was a decent enough wage for me at the time, and there was always a helpful amount of commission on top of my wages every month.

I started halfway through the month, that was the only month that I didn't outsell fellow staff. I was immediate competition for my colleagues, outselling both my senior and the sales manager became the norm. This confirmed selling really was my true profession, it would one day pay the mortgage on a very nice, detached, rural property, enable me to drive expensive German cars all my life, take the family on plenty of holidays each year, and put each of my kids through university.

I couldn't believe it, for the first time in my life, I was doing well professionally, everyone there knew me solely for being good at my job. I felt so proud, this feeling was new to me, this felt like the beginning of a promising career. Another first was that I truly enjoyed going to work, this felt very odd – but I loved it.

The split from the girlfriend happened some months before this point, just before that last lot of trouble. Following the split things did go downhill, as much as I thought of myself as being stable, self-sufficient, and entirely emotionally resilient, the split knocked me for six. She was an amazing person, so attentive, so helpful, so considerate, unbelievably patient, so understanding, literally the cornerstone of my life back then, I completely took her for granted and I'd lost her. She was working at this Hilton too, and now she had to put up with hearing how amazingly well I was doing, which couldn't have been very nice for her. Not because she didn't want me to succeed but, it's just not very nice is it, especially as I had not been a good boyfriend, putting it incredibly mildly, the split was down to me completely.

I was performing well at work, but outside of work I didn't know what to do with myself. The biggest problem was that my shifts were either 10-6.30 or 12-8.30, I would go out the night before and hit town way too hard for a school night. I was going out most nights, with absolutely anyone who I bumped into. Anything just to take my mind off her. One night I was pulled over by the police, not sure what for. They breathalysed me (standard procedure for everyone when pulled over), the limit is 35 and I blew 40-something, this initiated driving ban number 3.

Just like every other ban, I ignored this one too, I continued to drive myself to and from work which was about 25-45minute drive each way, dependent on route, time of day etc. On the rare occasion I would care about possibly getting caught, I would tell myself "Ok, I don't have a license, but I'm breaking the law for a decent reason", I'd convinced myself that the police, legal system and most importantly for me at the time, karma would be on my side.

The police knew me, the situation, my car, and by this point the police had developed knowledge of my habits, they knew where I parked it when in Cheddar. I didn't know this at the time – but was just about to find out. It was one of my days off, I was on my way home from the gym. I wasn't far from my chosen spot where I used to park, achieving keeping it "out the way" (I thought).

Literally, no more than 30 seconds left of the journey, before I would have reached the turning and parked up. When, blue lights appear in my rear-view, "handy!". I put my foot down, my parking spot was down a private lane right next to wear I was living at the time, I made it there, swung it in, parked up and legged it.

There was a route through the estate, to the public carpark next to the area's reservoir. It was a walk I'd done many times; I just about made it to the carpark, I was panting furiously, throat bone-dry, just before breathlessness got the better of me, I managed to ring a mate, "Quick come and get me." She drove over and picked me up and let me hide at her place.

The police always recover a vehicle that's been involved in anything, so they impounded it, leaving me with no way to get to work the next day. Alfie was up to date with everything concerning the newest driving ban so, lent me his pushbike. I had the pleasure of cycling to work, I thought I would enjoy a nice little 18-mile round bike journey to work and back, in any other job such a dramatic change like this may look somewhat suspect but when you work at a health club, simply claiming to be "keeping fit" was enough to both answer colleagues curiosity and eliminate any suspicion, if there ever was any.

The journey to work – yeah manageable, enjoyable in fact, along the "Strawberry Line" (one of those converted railway tracks). The journey home – "oh dear". It was always dark by the time I finished work. This bike didn't have any lights, and I couldn't afford any. As the journey along the cycle track was mainly crossing countryside, I only had the moon's light to illuminate the path, the journey was an absolute hazard, along the road was longer and much more dangerous especially in the dark without lights. I tried making the journey home on the bike maybe twice, before deciding 'I needed to find another way'.

A friend of mine who always liked to have the best of everything, had a Honda CRF 450 on Supermoto wheels, just an offroad bike that had been made to "look" road legal – simply done, by wiring up a headlight and a taillight - illuminating its false number plate, This particular bike had also had its engine professionally tuned. I said to him "When I get the BM back, fancy swapping it for that bike?" he agreed.

I'd always enjoyed motorbikes but only ever off-road, the last time I tried riding a motorbike on the road was that morning on my way to court, when I went through some poor bugger's fence. I had never had any interest in riding a motorbike on the road, simply because I knew that I couldn't trust myself. I would happily do off-roading all day long - if you come off it's a much softer landing surely, but never on the road, and that bike scared me. In either of the first 3 gears, pull back on the throttle and I'd be on the back wheel, it was a powerful bike, immense torque.

Paternity tests were about 300 quid back then and I couldn't afford that – no way. I was employed and earning but, every pay check was already spent before I'd even received it, remember those payday loans – I was on first name terms with those guys. After managing to clear enough debt, I finally had the money for a paternity test, so went and bought one at the first chance I got. After managing to arrange a time and place to meet and complete the relevant steps of the test, done and dusted I posted it straight away – T minus 3 weeks.

Life for me at that point was slowly but surely falling apart, all the progress I felt I had been making was dissolving away, right in front of me. I felt a silver lining had become clear, when I was told that an "opportunity" was about to present itself in work, for me specifically, this was an effective distraction from the mess that I'd created for myself. To anyone I saw or spoke to, it wouldn't have been even faintly apparent that I wasn't managing to hold it together. My life behind the scenes was spiralling out of control and was about to get a whole lot worse.

One Saturday evening I was at a friend's house with a couple of mates, nothing out of the ordinary. In the early hours of Sunday morning, having run out of alcohol and ciggies hours ago, we knew the shop would be opening soon so, we decided to make our way there.

We got there a bit too early but, not long to wait, so, we made ourselves comfortable on a bench not far from the shop. There was a bloke already sat there, no doubt doing the same as us. I had "near enough" sobered up by this point, "you know, when you're not falling over drunk, but tying your shoelaces would be an accomplishment". I wasn't really a smoker – only after a beer so, at this stage of the session, I was an enthusiastic smoker. I noticed this guy had just finished a fag, so politely asked him if he had one spare, he snapped at me, "not for you!" (I didn't know this at the time but, he knew me as I'd had 'altercations' with a couple of his friends in the past) I made a joke of it, "Aright, aright, calm down, calm down."

I turned away and carried on chatting. This guy was close enough for me to see out the corner of my eye that, for the next few minutes he just sat there staring at me, it felt as if he might have been trying to get a reaction, he didn't look away once.

His intentions had sort of become clear to me in my half-cut state, I turned to him and said, "look mate, please stop staring, you're really winding me up."

My mates were all "uwwww!" Winding the situation up. I turned away again, but he never stopped staring, then he stood up, his eyes still glued on me, I said "come on mate, let's not fall out."

I then, stood up too, a very brief physical 'disagreement' followed, he's now on the floor. It took a moment for the penny to drop, "ah shid, that'll breach that suspended sentence thing." I legged it and went to a mate's house nearby, let myself in and just crashed out on his sofa. I woke up hours later, and crept home to the other side of Cheddar.

The following morning, the police published a photo in the local paper and the areas Facebook page, a screenshot taken from the shop's CCTV of me looking through the shops entrance moments before the incident, facing the camera, head to toe, clear as day.

A day later, I was at my current residence, in my room on the top floor. First thing in the morning, I heard the doorbell go, for some reason I instantly thought "police!" My friend's mum is the nicest lady you've ever met. I could hear her inviting someone in. As the house was a large townhouse, staying out of sight whilst getting close enough to listen was easily achievable. I recognised the sound of some big boots walking over the tiled hallway floor, along with faint radio chatter, confirming it was police. I got that helpful panic, and started asking myself "Why are they here?" "What will they ask?" "What might they be looking for?" "What would they like to find? - what do I need to hide?" After having a quick panic tidy. I went downstairs acting completely oblivious.

"Alright?"

"Ah - Mr Sumner."

"Mornin', what's up?"

"We have reports of..." And he starts describing the incident from outside the shop. He said, "I need to have a look amongst your belongings".

I knew exactly what they were looking for. In the photo of me in the paper, I am wearing some very distinctive bright orange trainers and a black knee length parka, I thought that the police would like to find these items, so during my constructive panic, I had hidden both of these, in a different bedroom. The copper went up and had a look in my room, didn't find them, "Right, Okay, that's me done," and he left.

A few days later they called me, to tell me I was being summoned to take part in a police line-up. Following just a hint of panic, I thought "no problem, I'm well practised in misleading authorities" - or so I thought. I came up with a plan "I know, I'll wear my smart 3-piece, nobody around Cheddar has ever seen me dressed like that," I travelled there thinking "I don't look like Greg Sumner, I'm gonna ace this."

The way they do ID line-ups now, is they video you, get you to turn left and right, then they show the victim the recording.

I walked into the police station, and I think, because of the way I was dressed, I found they treated me with a whole new respect, not exactly holding doors for me but after being in this setting many times before it was noticeable.

When I walked into the video suite, they looked me up and down and they weren't happy, this technique obviously wasn't anything new to them.

"You'll need to put this on?"

Handing me this massive, oversized, scruffy, old jumper.

"Oh…"

A week or so later, I received a letter letting me know that I "had been positively Identified" and a date of when my case would be heard, "9$^{th\ of}$ October at Taunton crown Court" again. They had me on CCTV, I had been "formerly identified," they knew it was me, my luck had run out, no escaping it this time. That suspended sentence meant that I'd be going down for the original sentence of 4 years, plus whatever I'd get for this GBH. Even though this very concerning, ominous future was pretty-much definite, I wasn't that concerned, my thoughts were more, "ahh well, it's been a long time coming".

Remember that girl Abi, I bumped into at Sophies house, just after starting college? We hadn't spoken for years, I hadn't even seen her since Sophie's, as we didn't live near each other, different friendship groups etc. But around this time, we'd been talking well, messaging each other, good old social media. From conversation so far, we found that we were literally perfect for each other. Apart from the name, she was everything and more that I could have ever asked for. After that breakup leaving me in bits, I felt that Abi 'popping up' again was going to help me out of the hole I felt I was in. Honestly, this girl was wife material like you wouldn't believe. my type exactly. Yes, I know, I probably should have mentioned the recent incident, and the fact that I'd be going to prison in a minute, I just couldn't ever find the right time, I didn't want to spoil what I hoped was unfolding.

Chapter 8

Sunday October 7th, 2012

October 6th, 2012 was a Saturday, I was on the late shift, on my own at the Health Club, working from noon until 8.30pm. It had been a fairly slow, tedious day, things were quiet, so I'd spent most of the day tying up loose ends, setting myself up for another blinding week of sales. "Yes, I was going to be sent to jail the coming Tuesday but, as work didn't have even the slightest inkling that Greg was anything other than what they saw each day, I didn't want anything to appear 'out of the ordinary', I wanted to keep things going just like any other day, I think?"

As my shift came to an end, I planned to have a quick blast in the gym before heading home, I was on the early shift the following morning so I knew I had to distract myself from the fact that it was a Saturday night and town would be heaving.

I got home at about 10, just as planned, home – food – trackies – bed. I was on my bed, watching tv, I could feel my eyelids getting heavier and heavier then, "ding" a txt, it was Abi. She was just letting me know her plans for the evening. She wasn't really a "night out in Weston" kind of girl so, this was an invitation, 'yea work in the morning buuut'. I immediately put up a status, asking if anyone "fancied town" – I needed a lift. Not that she knew it yet but, she was about to be my girlfriend.

A friend commented, he was up for it, and volunteered to drive, he picked me up soon after and we made our way into town. We arrived in Weston-Super-Mare just before 11 and parked in the large supermarket carpark right in the centre, most of the town's nightlife, was just another five-minute walk from there. My sole intention that night was to find Abi but, didn't want to seem too keen, trying to play it cool. We called in at a few bars along the way, before eventually getting to where she said she'd be. I went and found her; we enjoyed ourselves into the early hours.

It got late; the alcohol had just about gotten the better of me, I'd lost Abi. Considering I had work in 8 hours, my common sense made an appearance - I decided I needed to go home. Located my mate, we mutually decided to call it a night.

Without any discussion or even slight hesitation, we automatically just walked back to his car. Why did we get in that car? We could have found someone going the same way, we could have gotten a taxi or phoned someone for a lift. But no, we just got in the car, neither of us even stopped to consider otherwise.

On our way back to the car, we had decided to get something to eat, we were going to pass a drive through on the way home "perfect, we'll call in there".

Whilst sat in the car eating our food. I'm glued to my phone texting Abi, being that drunk this required all my attention. Being so engrossed in my phone, I was oblivious to the disagreement that was unfolding between my mate and a group of lads in a car just a few metres away. Eventually, they drove off, we left the car park at the same time. Intending to chase/follow/race I've no idea?

I don't really remember the journey; I'd had a skin full, and I was too busy on my phone, fishing for an invite round to hers. I wasn't paying absolutely any attention to the route, journey, driving etc. Police reports do say that I flicked them the v's, I don't recall doing so, I'm not denying it, I don't doubt this for a second, a hand signal of that nature would've been pretty standard when seeing/meeting confrontation. It's clear we were not the lead vehicle at any point.

Following the car in front, took us on a much longer route, I've only learnt this through reading police reports, detailing the exact route. 25-30 minutes into the chase we were flying along the "Cheddar bypass" a mostly straight and very wide road into Cheddar.

There are only 5 roads into Cheddar, this was the main one and most familiar to both of us. We had both travelled this road thousands of times each over the years, either as passengers or drivers, we'd driven this route in vans, trucks, cars, bikes it was such a familiar road.

We flew past a taxi going the same way, at the speed we were traveling we were no more than 20 seconds away from where we would have passed a street that cut through to the road I lived on, and I would have said "I'll jump out here". We were coming up to a very mild left-hand kink in the road, not a corner, just a slight kink. We were going quick, way too quick, and as we took the bend, the size and weight of our vehicle combined with the speed we were traveling at, meant keeping the car on our side of the road just wasn't possible.

Deservedly, the next 100 yards will haunt me for as long as I live, at 2:48 exactly, on that Sunday morning, we were about to find out that there was a vehicle traveling towards us. The next few moments are going to leave four kids without dads, a wife, and a long-term partner without their other halves, 4 parents would lose a son each, the ripples go on and on.

Sunday, 7th October 2012, 2:48am - on the A371 just coming into Cheddar we crashed head-on. We were doing 90mph, the oncoming car was doing 40mph. It was being driven by a local man, who was a father of 2, on his way to work.

Both driver's lives were ended, the second the vehicles met.

Our car rolled, flipped, spun, whatever else and had come to a rest on its roof after leaving the road. That taxi we'd just overtaken was the first vehicle on the scene. Luckily, the driver had a fire extinguisher on board, and he valiantly kept the flames that kept igniting under control, while waiting for the emergency services to arrive. Within minutes, the local fire crew from Cheddar were on the scene, they quickly and easily established that my body was the only one still alive. Cheddar being a very close knit, little village in 2012, a few members of the fire crew were actually close friends of Alfie's, had been since they were toddlers, so knew me well too.

Due to being so severely disfigured, I was unrecognisable, until something distinctive of mine (trainers, watch, clothing) became visible. That was the moment that the fire crew realised whose body they were untangling from the wreck. They spent the next 60 minutes separating my body from the mangled metal.

Paramedics arrived moments after the fire crew. Throughout the recovery, they had to keep injecting me with adrenalin to maintain a pulse. As my circulatory system was such a mess, they had to drill a hole into a bone, to inject directly into the bone marrow, this was the only effective way of delivering a "full dose."

There is a hospital in W-s-M but anything major, was all dealt with in Bristol. Out of the 3 main hospitals in Bristol, the only one with room for a case of such severity was Frenchay, the furthest away of all 3, but as it was the only one with space – it had to be that one. I don't know how many doses of adrenalin I received, but the paramedics managed to keep my heart beating throughout the rescue and 30-mile journey. I was losing copious amounts of blood; I was quite literally hanging on by a thread. With every second that passed, I was getting closer and closer to death.

Once we got to Frenchay my case was prioritised, as the most severe of the emergencies waiting.

The most substantial of the blood loss was coming from my right leg. Flesh had been sliced off right down to and along the majority of my femur, luckily the artery had only been grazed, if the wound was just millimetres to the side, I would have bled to death within minutes, this was the most urgent injury as well as the easiest to fix. The open wound left from where the flesh had been sliced off, was far too wide to simply stitch up, the surgeons had to take a 2x7inch strip of skin from the inside of my thigh, to patch up the wound.

After being made as stable as possible, around 30 'give or take'. completely broken bones were found, there were breaks at either end of my spine. As well as the breaks, two of my vertebrae in my lower back had completely disintegrated. Most of my ribs were broken after meeting the impact of being caught by the seatbelt, both arms and forearms, wrist, legs, ankles, various bones in each of my hands and feet to name just a few, oh and annoyingly, I only have half of my pinky toe on my left foot remaining.

Considering all the injuries running the length of my spine, somehow my spinal cords were totally unaffected. The most serious injury of all, was caused by the devastating impact to my head. This caused what is termed (I kid you not) an A.B.I – acquired brain injury.

Whilst all this was happening the police are desperately trying to contact somebody of relevance, family etc. My ID had been recovered from my pocket, in the form of a driving license (I told the court I didn't have the physical license, the last time they banned me, this prevents them taking it, that ID is always preferable)

At the time of applying for my first license, my sister suggested that I list her salon as the address on the document, simply because I wasn't sure where I would be living when the physical license card would be delivered.

So, the address on all my licenses and therefore the polices first port-of-call was my sisters salon, the person in the property above heard the frantic, repetitive, knocking and went to investigate. Following their interaction, the police were given my brothers phone number. My brother was hosting an event close to Bath and after answering one of the many calls from the unknown number he instantly dropped everything, and rushed to Frenchay hospital to "identify the body they'd recovered." He's told me since, "you were so fluked up, I couldn't even tell it was you". Then he remembered that I had a tattoo on my right forearm. He asked someone to turn my arm over. The moment he could make out the resemblance of a tattoo, he knew that the mangled mess of a human in front of him was his little brother, he froze, he told me his heart stopped. He's admitted to me since that he "cried like a little beech", but he won't want me to put that, so yeah, don't anyone mention that bit to him.

Word had gotten round the family by now, my parents travelled from Kent and were next on the scene. Closely followed by James and his wife Kristie, who collected Abi from Chester on their way down from Yorkshire. Anna-Marie and Babs were in Spain at the time of the crash. They rushed back and were next to my bed in less than 48hours.

Despite being unconscious – for the first few days, my body/limbs would continuously thrash around uncontrollably, my temperature would fluctuate so rapidly to dangerous, life-threatening levels, I constantly needed transferring between a mattress filled with ice cold water and a specially heated one. This was only the beginning; things were bad and were going to get much worse. The severity of the brain injury was enough for Dr's to decide that an induced coma would be the most appropriate course of action, as the volatility of a body's reactions is greatly reduced when unconscious.

For the first few weeks of the coma, my body never stopped deteriorating, the stream of disturbing, distressing news and updates on my worsening condition was continuous.

Take a moment to put yourselves in a family members place; your continually being filled with reem's of terrifying medical terms and information about your child, nephew, little brother, and you can't do anything but stand and watch, as the loved one in front of you slowly dies.

Friends at both ends of the country, general public and my family in Canada all learnt about the crash over the following days, my good mate/old boss Julian organised church ceremonies, as well as other social occasions for well-wishers and mourners alike, attendees came from Weston-Super-Mare, Cheddar, Bristol, Taunton, Chester, and North Wales. I've spoken to various people who went, those there were already pretty much mourning my death, this was quite chilling to hear.

A considerable amount of surgery followed over the next few days.

One evening, around 3-4 weeks into the coma, my family were taken into a private room, "strange" they thought? It was nicely furnished/just not as drab as the usual hospital decor, there was a table and chairs, much more homely than the standard hospital waiting room. Anna-Marie noticed "there were boxes of tissues dotted around this room?" Once everyone had gotten comfortable and settled down very slightly, a doctor entered the room and very calmly let my family know my chance of survival was now just 30% and were told that "the chance of me regaining consciousness was becoming unlikely", this was the frightening reality of just how serious things were. I'd been unconscious for around 3 weeks, those volatile physical movements stopped ages ago, I didn't move by myself at all anymore, this was my brain shutting down. Around this time, those results from the DNA test had arrived at Anna-Marie's salon. Dad kept getting asked to open the envelope, as much as Dad wanted too, he said "no, not until Greg is with us." This was Dad trying his best to be optimistic.

Stabilising injuries of such severity was difficult, this level of horrifying, unpredictable, frightening, instability persisted for the first 6 weeks. The likelihood of never again being able to touch, hold, hug, see, their son, brother, nephew, ever again was an obvious and strong possibility.

I needed a team of nurses to keep me alive. As my heart was so weak it actually stopped beating, I had to be revived on 2 separate occasions. I developed sepsis (blood poisoning), as my liver had shut down, meaning my circulatory system had to be plumbed into a dialysis machine. Due to the severe impact to my head, I had to have a tiny electric device inserted through a hole and sat just within my skull, to measure exactly how much pressure there was between my throbbing, swollen brain and the wall of my skull. My face and jaw had been so badly broken, my airway wasn't clear so, I was breathing through a tracheostomy (artificial airway opening) and connected to a ventilator, this was breathing for me due to a punctured and collapsed lung.

Every unconscious body still needs nutrition, for this I needed a P.E.J (a tube passing through the wall of my stomach, to deliver nutrients to my lower intestine). Whilst a heart rate monitor kept a heartbeat, my organs were slowly shutting down. Oh and, I developed pneumonia, a few days into the coma, and would develop pneumonia again before waking up. But the icing on the cake, was catching MRSA, you know that infamous, infection that's resistant to antibiotics, not to worry – its only dangerous to those with a weakened immune system, 'GULP'! On the plus side, this infection meant I got my own room. #Living/notsolivingitup

I was meant to be in Taunton Crown Court for that GBH, the day after the crash, somehow CPS had been made aware that I hadn't shown due to being "unable to attend", they sent a couple of coppers up to the hospital, to check that this was the case. What they saw was enough for the CPS to instantly conclude that "it wasn't in the public's interest to pursue the case."

My family kept a daily diary of every little change during the ordeal, and it's noticeable that the entries become fewer and farther between after week 6. It must have been so hard for everyone who cared. I will never be capable of putting into words how grateful and sorry I am to all those concerned. As bad as things got, as daunting as everything looked my family never gave up hope.

At the approximate halfway point of the coma my family were gathered in my room, a doctor came in, visibly uncomfortable, everyone who was there agrees that everything about this Dr, the way he hovered into the room, spoke, carried himself all triggered memories of being told about my chance of survival. But this time, the doctor began by saying, "it looks like Greg is going to wake up, however, the injury to his brain was so severe that when he wakes, there is a significant chance that there won't be anything left of the

Greg you know, other than his appearance." An incredibly bitter pill to swallow but at the same time this, was some amazing news. Overall, this news cheered everyone up. Another slow month passed before it was deemed safe to start trying to wake me up.

Anyone in an induced coma is being kept unconscious using heavy sedation. So, when the time comes to wake the patient, it is done very gradually over days.

They would wake me up enough to see how my body would react, temperature, heartrate etc. But then they would have to put me under again after seeing the volatility of my fragile body's reactions, "1 step forward, 3 steps back". They would have to reset my sedation and wait for my body to relax, before trying again a couple of days later. After declaring it safe to wake me up, the third attempt was successful, "bringing me round," took 9 days altogether.
After regaining consciousness enough to open my eyes, the most severe confusion engulfed me immediately. Desperately trying to work out where I was and what was going on. I was led down in a bed, "why am I in bed?" I gathered I couldn't move anything but, this didn't concern me there and then. My head was completely scrambled, I could see that I was in a small room that to me, resembled some sort of medical facility, but I had my very own room? 'Naah, this isn't hospital, I've got my own room and feel fine.'

As soon as I could pay attention to who was in the room, dads was the first face I focused on. He didn't look happy or unhappy, just kind of satisfied? I didn't have the faintest clue what was going, or had gone on? I tried to say something, but nothing came out, I kept trying but, nothing? Again, this didn't really concern me either? I was overwhelmed by confusion.

"This may sound like those present were just leaving me to sweat it out, of course they weren't. The above took no more than a handful of seconds."

Dad could see that I was trying to talk, so promptly drew my attention to my neck and started talking – he would have obviously been explaining why I couldn't talk but, I wasn't listening, my poorly brain was panicking, desperately trying to make sense of the situation. There were some others next to dad, upon focusing I could see that Jen, Babs, Alfie and Kathryn was there also, everyone else looked just as content as dad, but slightly more excited? Kathryn had tears running down her face but, she wasn't upset, she actually looked quite happy?

The first thing dad did after a brief update (brief as instructed by professionals; to avoid upsetting/startling me) was, he opened that envelope, read the contents and then told me that the letter confirmed that I was a father. I could hear him perfectly fine and understood every word he'd just said. In the same way that I knew the faces in the room - I recognised this subject too. I could feel this was some good/positive/exciting, news. My head was busy doing summersaults, as I've said I did recognise this subject – I didn't yet know the ins and outs, my mind was incapable of concentration. Looking back, I think Dad did this to figure out just how much of his son was left.

Dad had been asked several times, to open these results, but he had insisted on waiting until I woke. Even though my family were told that I mightn't ever wake, Dad stuck to his wishful positivity, Dad's optimism carried the family.

After opening the results, communication was the most immediate issue. Dad held up a card with the alphabet printed on it and explained to me that he would go through the letters, and I had to nod when he got to the relevant character to spell out the word. After Dad had explained the function of the alphabet card thing a couple more times, I thought I understood it enough to make use of it and I really tried, I just couldn't handle the rage, that resulted from failing to understand. It was just as painfully slow, as it was infuriating. I knew exactly what I wanted to say but, after sustaining such a severe brain injury – my spelling/comprehension most certainly 'needed some work'. That, and I just didn't completely understand the concept enough to utilise it.

On a separate visit, a couple of days after I'd woken, when everyone told me they were going, and I should "get some rest"; this angered me, and I really upset Anna-Marie by singling her out when making this known, I thought they had only been there two minutes, but they had actually been there just under 12 hours, I had only been awake for a small portion of their visit.

Obviously, there was a great deal going on, but I had no idea, 'ignorance is bliss'. The following few days/weeks sort of merge into one big blur.

Following seeing the news the night before and learning of the date and therefore the severity of the situation, right from the moment dad arrived the next morning, I started furiously interrogating him as best I could in my broken English. Dad had obviously been anticipating questions of this nature. "Where's my mate?" "What happened?" "Why can't I move?" "When will my body work?" "Am I paralysed?" He told me that, my friend hadn't survived, briefly went over the crash and that I was not "paralysed", but because of the blow to the head, the connection between my brain and my muscles was not working.

A week or so passed, I learned more about my injuries and what I had been through since the crash. The coma, pneumonia, organ failure, MRSA. I had come close to dying several times. I learnt not only had my friend not made it, but there was another vehicle involved, the sole occupant of which had also been killed. "There was someone else involved?" this made everything a great deal worse.

After I'd been awake for some time, unrelated visitors were permitted to visit in person. First of which was my son's mum, accompanied by her mother. Alfie's mum came in first, looking sort of blank/emotionless, not in a nasty way, thinking about it – finding the right facial expression for that scenario can't have been easy for anyone? Her mum followed her in, and the moment she laid eyes on me, she turned round immediately and left the room. She only left briefly before re-entering, I can only imagine that the sight of me, must've been difficult to take in, especially as she had only ever seen the athletic, gym mad, healthy Greg. Either that or maybe she'd just forgotten something. I don't remember anything of the interaction that followed.

A range of different visitors came over the next couple of months. As the story of my struggle had been so widely publicised, I often didn't know or even recognise visitors, I think, there was a portion of people who'd just read or heard about my story and wanted to see "poor Greg" for themselves. I was normally always in a state of confusion and couldn't talk, so I just reacted as if pleased to see everyone, whether I knew them or not. Not being able to talk was often a blessing in disguise, nobody presses for conversation, when you can't speak. Even if I could have spoken, I wouldn't have said anything of any value, my head was just blank, not totally blank, my mind could only think about what was happening at that exact moment in time, I couldn't anticipate or reflect. You could have told me the craziest, most unimaginable rubbish you could think of, I would've just smiled and nodded.

I can see how some might think this would have been alarming/frightening – but for me, at that point, I didn't have the ability to have an opinion, the mental incompetence meant I was oblivious to everything, I think my inability to understand shielded me from the ongoing. Another blessing in disguise.

I had brother Alfie with me all day most days, he barely ever left, Despite the severity of the whole situation, thoughts like "what's on tv?" were probably the most crucial of my concerns. There was very little else going on in terms of mental activity.

After being awake for some time, physios began visiting. Not being able to move voluntarily, meant that the physio sessions were just, having my stiff, tender joints moved manually. This was the physio evaluating what ability remained. I didn't enjoy these visits, on the plus side even though these sessions were always same day and time, with the exact same staff, because I couldn't retain information, by the time the next session came around, I'd have absolutely no idea what was about to happen, it was something new to me every time.

My very first experience of seriously painful physio, happened soon after visitors had been permitted. Jason, the manager of the Health Club called in, coincidently moments before one of these physio sessions began.
I found myself being lifted out of bed, with what I recognised as some sort of engine crane, (it was a hoist, at this point I'd never seen one of these before.) Despite having watched them prep a wheelchair and being hoisted out of bed I was incapable of putting 2 and 2 together. Even if I had been able to cobble together a question, I had no speech so couldn't have asked it anyway. I was lifted from my bed and lowered into a standard wheelchair. It probably had adequate padding, but sitting on what was left of my bum was unbearable. I had lost so much weight throughout the coma, that the cushioned

seat felt like a lump of granite. It felt like the bones in my bum were about to pierce through the skin. Poor Jason was stood there trying to present me with a gift and card, I just sat there silently bawling my eyes out, with a face to match the level of pain – mouth wide open, streaming with saliva, I could not talk, I could not call for help, I couldn't do anything, I just sat there in floods of tears over the excruciating discomfort. After a couple of minutes in the chair, which felt like a lifetime, the physios came back, and I was hoisted back onto the bed. This was a very mild first taste of just how painful life was about to become.

Chapter 9

Moving on

May/June 2013

The day came for me to move on from the intensive care unit to HDU (High Dependency Unit). This was just across the corridor, literally directly opposite Intensive Care but, considering how devastatingly grim things had gotten whilst in ITC, for my family it felt like serious progression, I was still extremely ill, but at long last, it was actually a step in the right direction.

Even though, I hadn't had MRSA for quite some time, it was still deemed necessary for me to have my own room. It was here, that I showed the first signs of thinking for myself, unfortunately I did this through finding problems, and being generally downbeat, constantly annoyed, which always resulted in intoxicating frustration.

The most upsetting issue to me regarding the move, was the fact that my curtains in the new room didn't match, one of them was about 6 inches too short, because this issue was within eyesight this meant I unintentionally focused way too much attention on the matter.

Obviously, Dad was the first to hear of this, he reassured me "don't worry about that, the rooms décor is very minor in the grand scheme of things", Dad said this straight faced with a tone, whilst tilting his head forwards, almost patronising if you don't know Dad, "I recognise that!" This was dad's way of getting whoever just spoke to pay attention to what they'd just said, "yeah, not that important I suppose…".

It was here where I saw my boy Alfie for the first time since waking up. I had the tracheostomy so I couldn't talk, he was only a toddler, so he couldn't really talk much either but, I enjoyed it none-the less.

I still had brother Alfie with me most days, looking back, I don't know what I would have done without him there. Just having someone with me whilst segregated from the hospital population, to share my usually always incorrect and heavily misguided thoughts, ideas and theories with, who would then correct, rationalise and/or apply logic to my endless stream of confused nonsense, this helped to disrupt the constant, exhausting, dull, depressing stream of nasty, punishing thoughts, that and funnelling way too much of his money into my pay as you go hospital TV.

Alfie, being Alfie, one day took a load of girly pictures out of *various* magazines in the room (visitors often brought these as gifts) and kindly covered the wall I was facing with them. Many of the nurses were from different cultures/backgrounds and didn't appreciate my brothers interior design efforts.

One day, soon after Alf's artwork, I was on my own, 2 of the nurses came in, and without saying a single word to me, had a brief chat in their own language whilst facing this wall, then just started tearing the pictures down. Without any consideration of me whatsoever, the old Greg wouldn't have even hesitated before "pouncing", he certainly would have made his feelings very well-known, stopping them before they'd even start, but I was so tired, worn-out, completely, entirely drained mentally and emotionally, that I just lay there watching them do it. I could well have made enough of a commotion to get their attention but, I just didn't have it in me, I couldn't even consider summoning the strength, effort, energy to protest. "What's the point? They're not bothering to ask because I'm so pathetic and obviously don't matter anymore". This was me most of the time now, I just didn't have any fight in me, nothing whatsoever. This brought me down so much more, this now clear helplessness really hurt, I felt so insignificant. Later, when telling/moaning to dad, he reminded me that, there were far more important things to get upset about, he said this empathetically, to reassure me.

I was on the HDU for about 4/5 months, throughout that time my level of morale never stopped plummeting. Thankfully, Alfie was still with me so much. All my days here sort of merge into one period, my number of visitors dropped dramatically here, but that issue was about to sort itself.

Chapter 10

Rehab begins
2013

HCA's, Nurses, Physio's "I've no idea, could've been Mr Blobby for all's I knew/cared," came into my room one day and started getting me/things ready, before transferring me onto a smaller bed (it was a stretcher), I didn't know what was going on, as per I just gormlessly went along with it, I was then taken off the ward.

I was loaded into the back of an ambulance. This was all new to me, I had only ever been in an ambulance after the crash, and I wasn't particularly "observant" on that occasion so, this time I was just taking it all in. I should have expected this trip, no-doubt I would have had it all explained to me, several times by a few different people but as retaining information wasn't a strong point, all this came as a very unexpected surprise.

In the same grounds as the Hospital was/is a rehabilitation unit. They were very selective about who they would accept, fortunately my case matched their precise line of work, Dad was the driving force behind my admission, he applied, and I was accepted. This was to be where my rehabilitation would begin.

This facility was spread over a large ground floor. The main entrance opened into the reception area; this was the hub of the building. Then there were 2,3,4 (not sure) long, perfectly straight corridors, running out from the hub. I don't remember much else regarding the layout, my brain couldn't remember exactly which room was where besides, when your being pushed in a wheelchair – you don't even need to consider navigation.

Upon arrival I was wheeled straight to my new room on the stretcher, transferred onto my own bed then left alone.

Shortly after getting there, Dad, Jen, Anna-Marie, Kathryn and Alfie joined me, they had a few gifts to help me settle. Now that I had my own room, they got me a tv, as well as some, cartons of orange juice and clothes – (they were pyjamas) so I could get out of wearing hospital gowns, getting to wear my own clothes was only a very minor change, but felt amazing. We were all feeling so happy, hopeful and optimistic. I was finally where I needed to be, feeding off everyone's excitement I felt amazing, we all did, the feeling of positivity was intense, this place would be my first step on the road to getting back on my feet, this place was going to be the solution.

Since I woke up from the coma, during my time in ITC + HD, whenever thirsty I was only ever permitted to suck the moisture from a small sponge on the end of a stick, after dipping it in water. The tracheostomy wasn't any concern, it was just that my swallow hadn't been "officially assessed". I don't think you could ever appreciate the frustration this created, this drove me crazy, feeling thirsty happened infrequently, but when it did happen, honestly a mouth full of baking flour would have been refreshing.

Following all the happy fuss and commotion, we were all feeling great. I had developed a thirst, through a series of gestures I let someone know I was thirsty, I had been asking for a proper drink for months, on this occasion we had all gotten a bit carried away in the moment, nobody thought to stop and remind me that I still had to wait for an assessment, everyone conveniently forgot. 'Surely one of those small cartons would be ok, after all it's not like I'd ever had any trouble swallowing saliva or that fluid from the sponge'.

Somebody had gotten the carton ready with the straw and began moving towards me, there I was frantically nodding away, beaming ear to ear, as the drink was getting closer. It got close enough for me to reach the straw, I latched on and began gulping furiously, 'this felt odd'? The sensation was brand new to me? It was just a kind of light tickle halfway down my throat, "kind of like when a drop of fluid goes down the wrong way", I felt like I needed to cough or at least have a bit of a splutter, by no means alarming, more so just irritating to begin with, not enough to stop me drinking. This was only a small carton, so I managed most of it before the tickle became too much, and I had to stop.

My poor family in the room, this must have been scary. Upon stopping, I coughed and spluttered until there was no air left inside me, by which stage I was completely incapable of inhaling. I just had to wait for my lungs to catch up with the choke and become able to inhale. This left me sat there silent and motionless with a ridiculous look on my face – paused "mid-choke", gradually turning purple. This pause would have lasted around 6-7 seconds. Obviously, nothing of any concern to the average joe – but considering my physical fragility since the crash, yeah this had everyone on their toes. After managing to compose myself, the acidity of the juice meant I brought it straight back up, covering my chest. We all froze, this was my first ever tap on the shoulder, reminding me that I was by no means even close to being "out of the woods".

That evening would be my first night there, I can remember becoming incredibly angry/annoyed. They wouldn't close my door or turn my light out, I'm almost positive that nobody explained anything at all? I couldn't understand why they were doing this, and because I still had the tracheostomy – I couldn't even ask. There was a member of staff sat at my door facing away from me, I was desperate to get their attention, they were no more than a few metres away, trying this whilst remaining almost entirely still and without your voice, "tricky!" That wound me up something fierce. It was horrible, I had no idea why this was being done, I couldn't make any sense of it, being so physically unable rendered me completely and utterly helpless, amplifying my frustration and fuelling some severe rage.

By the time I'd move from 1 place to the next, I would've forgotten this detail and the torment would reoccur, therefore I would make this same complaint to my parents the morning after my first night, they would repeat "it's because they need to do checks blah blah blah"

"Oh yeah…"

This was my introduction to the anger brought on every time my helplessness caused a "situation." That coupled with the bitter stress of being totally physically unable, will get the better of me many times, in every single institute. Gradually, I would push myself to learn a way of managing this mental state, I had to, the mental torment of "situations" would get to be too much, but unfortunately this wouldn't happen for a few long, grim, gruelling years yet.

Just a day after the move, I had my tracheostomy removed. This was incredible, for me, this was the first actual physical progress that I can personally recall. As my swallow still hadn't been assessed, I was still being fed liquid food through the P.E.J.
I had not actually spoken for nearly a year and could now finally talk. My voice was completely foreign to me. I didn't sound anything like I used to, my voice had no pitch, just a very slow, flat toneless drone, but I had so much to say! The change in day-to-day life that came with this and the move i.e. not just lying in bed all day, every day,

meant seeing more happening, meeting more people, hearing and actually taking part in different kinds of conversation, this did my mental state the world of good. But most importantly, a massive disruption between me and the alone time spent in my seriously annoyed, confused, debilitating headspace.

It took a couple of days for them to get me booked in and sort my timetable. My family were excited, and after feeding off their excitement – I was too. Talk of me getting back on my feet was frequently the topic of discussion between family, visitors and myself, it was aways spoken of as 'the next step', containing my excitement wouldn't have been possible even if I'd have tried.

So, first on the list was S.A.L.T – Speech and Language Therapy. My therapist was called Geri. She was the driving force behind getting my tracheostomy taken out so promptly, enabling me to get started straight away, "hit the ground running" - sort of thing.

Geri was Australian, I remember always trying to say "Geraldine" in what I thought would sound like an Australian accent, but upsettingly, I couldn't do accents anymore, so I've no idea what it actually sounded like. I'll never forget the very first exercise, Geri, said to me, (whilst brandishing a spirometer) "Royt Greg, brith in as dip as you can, 'n' then blaw into this mayt" (sorry/not sorry oz) - I thought, 'Are you joking? My breathing's not the problem?'

"Go!" so I blew the absolute entirety of my lungs out, as hard as my body would allow. The reading on the device was pathetic. As the ventilator had been breathing for me, for so long, the depth of my breaths was now astonishingly shallow, I had the lung capacity of a toddler.

I don't really remember anything else done in S.A.L.T as I said, after being mute for so long, I had so much to say. These sessions for me felt like just having a good chinwag with a mate, I felt that we were genuinely building a solid friendship. From the discussions we had, I believed she had a real interest in me, my welfare, my life, my entire story. No staff had ever before taken the time to talk with me like she did.

I wouldn't realise this for another couple of years but, she was just doing her job and getting me to talk.

"Oh…"

Every now and then she would go missing for "a while", (not sure how long for, my level of cognition coupled with my erratic sleep pattern, meant that I didn't really have any concept of time, could've been a day or a week). I couldn't work out where or why she'd gone, her whereabouts completely baffled me. "Where's she gone?" "Is she ever coming back?" "Maybe somethings happened, why doesn't anyone else care?" "I hope she's ok." Looking back now, obviously, these were just weekends! Yes, feels stupid to say now but, these unexplained absences really used to worry/upset me. If I'd have just thought to ask her or any other member of staff, this issue would have been so easily resolved but, my brain couldn't/wouldn't/didn't think of doing that, it would be another handful of years before I would get the hang of voicing queries, asking questions etc.

To begin with every part of physical rehab', was done in the hydro pool. Mon-Fri, I would get to spend a session in the amazing 38-degree water every day, so good, incredibly warm, honestly much more like a nice cosy bath, I loved my hydro sessions for this reason alone. The physios used the buoyancy to explore just how much strength, flexibility etc they had to work with – not that I knew this, to me I was just indulging in the warmth, I just saw "Hydro" as another chance to have a chat. These sessions began on my bed, being changed into my swimming shorts, then I would be transferred onto a "wet stretcher" (this term perplexed me, 'is it made from water?' until I saw it – just a mesh stretcher on wheels). After being taken to the hydro-pool I would then be hoisted from the stretcher and lowered into the water. I couldn't think of any practical purpose behind anything I ever did, I wasn't even curious? On the very rare occurrence, a question popped up in my head, just like always I wouldn't ever think to run-it-by anyone, I would come up with the answers on my own, unknowingly exercising my severely broken logic.

As much as I loved hydro', I really suffered when getting out of the water. Having lost so much weight and having no voluntary movement to generate body heat, any slight drop in temperature results in the most unbelievably intense shivering. The only muscles that worked/work were/are from the shoulders up, so only my jaw could/would shiver - violent chattering took over, the second I'd leave the water. They'd shower me, dry me, transfer me back to bed, dress me, then leave me to warm-up, this part of the process was always grim. Just like physio in ITC, even though they did this daily, the process always came as a surprise.

My time here was broken up by frequent visitors, my favourite of which were when my son Alfie came. He was just a toddler, so was always content with whatever we did, whether that be just sitting on my knee in the garden area or exploring my room.

Every time I did hydro, I would pass the "gym," so kept seeing fitness machines, not usual gym kit, just equipment that resembled stuff I used to use. I didn't yet know what to expect but in my head, I would be thinking "pfft, that's not proper gym stuff, I'll do all that with ease" but, as none of my muscles worked anymore, those machines would never be of any use to me, I needed reminding of this often, even though I couldn't even tense whatever muscle tissue remained, the reality of my situation wouldn't sink in for quite some time.

After hydrotherapy, the next step was to introduce physio in the "gym." My ears perked up immediately when I started hearing talk of a gym, in my head getting me back on my feet was finally about to begin, now that a gym was being introduced. But when I got there - it was unbelievably deflating. I'd been a persistent, and enthusiastic gym goer for the last 4 years before the crash, not exactly a lifelong commitment I know, but more than enough to form the opinion 'this is no gym'. It was just a room with a couple of machines (literally 2) and a handful of matts spread across the floor. Obviously, it wouldn't have ever had even the slightest resemblance to any gym that I'd ever used but, as I hadn't yet realised my situation, in my head I was still "old Greg". I wouldn't realise "new Greg's" physical limitations for another few years.

Within the next 6 weeks, my time at this place would come to a premature end. Daily physiotherapy was now the only rehab I did. Quite soon after starting in their 'gym,' I started feeling a dull ache in my lower spine. A month or so passed, and the pain had been constantly developing.

I'd always enjoyed the physical strain and the pain that followed a decent "gym sesh", putting this pain in that category enabled me to endure hours and hours of it. I just kept telling/reminding myself 'no pain, no gain' (my usual approach to the gym). Thinking about it, it wasn't anything even close to post-workout pain, after a good workout the feeling is always muscular, this felt deep within the bone, my brain just couldn't tell the difference.

Putting two and two together the professionals assumed that the cause of the pain must be something to do with the two false vertebrae, in place of those destroyed in the crash.

I would rely completely on what I was told, if somebody said that my spine was now made from strawberry jelly, as long as their speech was clear enough, I'd accept this – no question.

On a particularly bad day, I'd have to cut a session short and go back to bed. On the occasions the pain got the better of me before a session, someone would inform the physio, who would come to evaluate the situation, and then declare it "unwise to endure the strain of physio." The frequency of this pain kept increasing, as did the severity.

The puzzle of the back pain distracted all of us from the cough that had been steadily developing. What had started as a very occasional splutter, soon enough had turned into relentless, heavy coughing fits, all day, every day. It just kept getting worse, at its worst I couldn't manage any more than a few breaths between fits. One day, someone picked up on the cough, "oh yeah, now you mention it…".

The physical side of the fits took everything out of me. Not only did this exaggerate the existing pain in my spine, but the fits were now so constant that I couldn't even sleep, the exhaustion amplified the strain, my head would throb, in sync with each cough. I was in pain all over, head to toe - ringing out in a constant intense sharp-ache. Absolutely any sleep was impossible, I felt so tired, weak, pathetic, completely drained physically, mentally, emotionally, I was lifeless. I couldn't eat enough either, it's a good job staff opted to leave my P.E.J in place, this was now the only way to get nourishment into my body. It had gotten so bad that it was decided, I needed to go back over to the hospital. "1 step forward 5 steps back".

The rehab' was no more than a couple hundred metres from the hospital, but because it was a totally separate institute, an ambulance had to transport me. My dad arrived to visit, and was immediately approached by the manager, who explained that I needed to go back over to the Hospital, Dad agreed. Following a very calm and composed discussion, the manager then let Dad know of the reason for the wait, "excuse me?" This was not ok with Dad. If his son was unwell enough to need hospital, he wanted me to be seen to now, not "when they got round to it," especially as the hospital was so close. This frustrated Dad enough for him to come to my room, get my bed with me in it (hospital bed on wheels), intending to take me over to the hospital himself, he was told that "this was not and would never be permitted". I have never known dad to ignore authority but, he marched me straight out their front door and over there in the bed himself. "Done!"

A diagnosis of pneumonia was given, I was taken into a theatre almost immediately, I got another tracheostomy, "thank you, thank you, thank you!" this put an end to the torturous coughing fits instantaneously, "phew, relief." Following this modification to my airway, I slept solidly for about 6 hours, this mightn't sound much but this was easily over quadruple the length of a normal sleep. I was put on their most aggressive course of antibiotics; this would get rid of the most immediate symptoms.

Whilst in Frenchay Hospital this time, I was part of the actual ward as opposed to being in my own room. I didn't have a tv, so I just sat there watching the world go by, my broken brain never stopped trying to make sense of my paralysis, I thought, and confidently believed, 'If I surprised my body, it'll kind of react instinctively and wake-up'. One day, one of my bedrails had been left down, I spent all my effort, energy, and will, sort of wriggling, squirming, edging across the bed, intending to get close enough to the edge to slide off, thinking 'that'll wake me up!' Thankfully, a few inches before getting both shoulders over the edge the nurse came to do my meds, saw the issue and straightened me up. "Damn!"

When scanning me whilst investigating the pain in my spine, they were surprised to find big stones in my kidneys, stones of this size and very awkward shape are known as "staghorn calculus." Upon finding these, Doctors confirmed "these sizable kidney stones were the reason behind the debilitating back ache," it wasn't the damage to my spine after all, win-win, "pfft".

This meant I was going to need more surgery, I was okay with that, I just wanted to get back over there and get on with my rehab. The problem was, they didn't do the procedure for stones like these at Frenchay, so I was going to need to go to Southmead Hospital – on the other side of Bristol. So, another ambulance journey, another hospital.

This visit to Southmead lasted about 8 weeks, I was on the "Male Gastro" ward, where they dealt with everything bowel related. This was only my 2nd time on a ward.

Because of the problems this ward dealt with, it absolutely stunk. The hospital in general looked very tired and worn, this place was grim there and then. Thankfully dad and Jen were never too far away, Dad and Jen visited at least twice a day, the company was always nice, but at this hospital their time with me was essential. As the maximum vocal volume I could manage, was that of a new-born kitten, and being so incapable physically, I wasn't able to summon help. In bed 24/7, anything I wanted, a wee etc, I would need to wait for their visit – they were my voice. Yes of course, HCAs would come round the room a few times a day, but as my ability to remember was pretty much non-existent, the chance of me being prepared, and ready to ask for whatever it was that I needed/wanted, at the exact point they were passing, was equal to the chance of me doing the can-can.

I just like anybody else enduring a hospital visit of any similar length or nature, was required to have a cannula, cannulas are normally inserted into a vein on the inside of the elbow. (A cannula is a tube for insertion into the body to draw or introduce medication/fluid, to save needing to make a new hole each time) – "yea googled that, would've taken me ages to explain."

But because of my recent and extensive hospital interaction, nearly all my easily accessible veins, had already been used and were now "tired." A solution had been found; it had been decided that my cannula would be introduced into the large vein on the side of my neck.

I heard the term "local anaesthetic," I swear to you, I thought, "local anaesthetic? Oh, it must be made somewhere nearby", yeah, that was the state of my brain.

After the procedure being explained, to most talk of blades, necks and needles might sound a tad alarming, but me in my brain injured state, I didn't even have an opinion. When the time came, my bed was wheeled to the closest operating theatre, we didn't go into the actual theatre, the "scrub room" (where surgical staff dress for theatre) is always equally sterile, so that is where the procedure would be done. I had never been conscious through any "procedure" before, so I was busy taking in all the new sights, sounds, smells etc. Suddenly without any warning, the sharpest pain, I'm quite sure' I'd ever experienced in my entire life, completely out of the blue, it was the scalpel slicing my skin. Even though the cut was only small, it was incredibly painful, it was over in a couple of very uncomfortable minutes then, I was returned to the ward, Dad and Jen had waited for me.

Afterwards, I noticed that several Dr's seemed to be taking it in turns to come and inspect my neck. This appeared to be normal practice at first, but then I noticed that after their inspection, they would go just out of earshot and talk amongst themselves, whilst looking directly at me. Eventually the Dr's came to my bed to speak to Dad, I couldn't hear what was being said, this didn't bother me I knew that Dad would put whatever they'd said into terminology I'd understand. Their conversation finished, Dad came to me and said, "right, they need to redo your cannula," the student surgeon had made a mistake." This angered me, I got Dad to request a qualified surgeon this time, it was over quick, successful and was almost painless.

One of the mornings on this dingey, tired, smelly old ward, I'd woken up in discomfort, miraculously I'd managed to let a nurse know during "morning meds". After letting a nurse know, the information is always handed over to Dr's, discussed, dealt with, and handed over between staff when shifts change. As I'd let them know, my issue was "in the system" so the staff would come to me and ask about the issue specifically. The discomfort had developed into substantial pain by early afternoon. The "higher ups" were aware and had been discussing my rising pain level, they had come up with a solution.

A group of young student Dr's arrived at my bedside, to share their intended remedy. "To resolve your pain Mr Sumner, you're going to need a suppository".

I thought – 'I haven't heard that word before?' I'm practically a human pin cushion at this point in my life, how bad could another injection be? "Yea whatever, another injection, ready when you are".

"This isn't an injection Mr Sumner."

"Ey…?"

The very second, I learnt what a suppository was, I refused it immediately. I was thinking, "No, never ever in my life would I even consider the possibility of this". Coincidentally, my parents arrived shortly after this ridiculous proposal, I frantically repeated the outrageous suggestion I'd just heard. Even though Dad and Jen kind of managed to rationalise their suggestion, I was of course, still well and truly against it. The level of pain never stopped increasing, eventually it had gotten to the point I had difficulty breathing in rhythm, no exaggeration – imagine you're in excruciating pain throughout your torso, your spine feels similar to molten-lava, you're so desperate to just turn on your side and curl up but, the closest you can get, is to raise the head of the bed 30°. As I'd already exhausted every single available oral and intravenous pain killer, the intoxicating pain meant I was left no other choice. "Get the Doctor."

I didn't know this at the time but, the rehab' at Frenchay weren't going to let me back in. Their policy was that each patient only gets six months funded by the NHS, anything after that would need to be paid for. I was around 3 months in before being readmitted to Frenchay, so Dad wanted the remaining 3 months but, as there was no sign of them being able to get me working again, they said no to my return.

I moved from Southmead to what would be nursing home 1 of 2, CG. Dad got me excited, he had me feeling good about this place. following a brief trip in a private ambulance I met Dad and Jen there. My room was massive and sure enough all my photos of friends, and the "old Greg" were soon put up on the wall, I was satisfied here to begin with.

It was always so quiet, still, utterly motionless. After a couple of weeks, that torturous, lonely, punishing frame of mind had not only crept up on me again but, had worsened considerably and now dominated all available headspace. I found this place so depressing, after a month or so, the penny dropped; 'I'm a resident in a nursing home.' It was just a nursing home for the elderly. This realisation had a severely detrimental knock-on effect, my temperament had already begun heading downhill and never stopped deteriorating. I don't mean to be morbid, but this place was God's waiting room.

I had a few visitors each week – mostly family or Julian with the odd exception. I never got out of bed for any visits, I'd lay in bed 24 hours a day – 7 days a week – most weeks, my time in bed was only ever broken up by the odd, brief trip out with Alfie. The rest of the time, all day, every day, I was in bed. My son Alfie only visited here once, this was where I'd started telling myself "How unfair it was to put a small child through these visits", this was easier than endlessly thinking-up excuses for him being 'unavailable'.

I don't think my family particularly liked visiting here but, they would never make this even faintly apparent, ensuring my contentment was my families most important priority. A constant flow of visitors effectively distracted me from 'life' so, family did their best to ensure the flow was as constant as possible by working out a rota for visits between themselves.

Despite getting the regular doses of multiple different pain killers, I was still constantly in immense pain, it felt like head to toe, intense sort of growing pains, I would frequently summon the nurse (with the help of my nurse call button - a large button on the end of a flexible rod, to nudge with my head) I would then ask for a dose of the much heavier pain killer, Ora-morph.

At the time my family was told, "the level of daily pain was from a mixture of things; my body adjusting and getting used to all the foreign bodies (bits of metal holding bones together), breaks in bones resetting, along with all the scar tissue both internal and external".

On top of the above, a new kind of guttural pain started, but in these early days the pain was nothing in comparison to the rest, so it never got much attention. At this point in time, due to that bump on the head a little while ago, I could only manage to tell someone that I was in pain – then answer "yes or no" to questions regarding, I was unable to describe/explain, the kind or even the precise location of pain.

By now, I'd woken from the coma nearly 2 years ago and my brain had recovered an unhelpful amount, enough for my imagination to elaborate on the semi-built, understanding of what had happened, that I had put together myself over the years.

"Filling in the blanks", following a brain-injury of such severity, encouraged and then emphasised a strong sense of fear, along with a relentless feeling of definite impending doom. This really frightened me, I understood that I had reached my "end", remember those "Final Destination" films – exactly like that. I thoroughly believed this and would spend most of my time in this alarming mental space. Not that I had any idea at the time, but my understanding was obviously completely fictional, and because I would never share my thoughts, I would always fill in the blanks on my own – considering the wild, illogical, imaginative state of my thought's this was as reassuring as using google to self-diagnose something very minor.

These kinds of thoughts, along with being utterly incapable of processing them got me to my lowest mentally, unfortunately, anger was my only available emotion – my time here got really dark, this would have been obvious, I fell out with family, the few friends that bothered, visitors in general, staff, anyone and everyone I came into contact with, the toxicity of my bitterness was at its most potent here, about anything and everything. I was so angry, I hated life, I well and truly despised myself.

A very brief, but well needed ray of sunshine came along when my very good mate Adam, from primary school paid me a visit.

He'd arrived and was sent to my room, he entered my room as delicately as he could, for some reason he wouldn't look directly at me, and gave me a constant running commentary on everything as he entered the room. "Arite Greg it's Adam, from Northophall – I've come to visit, I'm coming in the room, now I'm closing the door...", I could hear him perfectly fine and understood everything he said, he was obviously treating me/the situation this way through fear of doing something wrong. It was just me and him; he was clearly nervous/uncomfortable/apprehensive, I'm not surprised to be fair. Seconds after making it through my door, that thing where I sort of choke on a drop of saliva happened, I erupt into an intense sort of cough/splutter, whilst desperately trying to make eye contact to reassure him.

"Thinking about it, the look on someone's face mid-choke wouldn't reassure anyone would it?"

This was enough for little Adam to panic bless him, throw the door open and start whaling down the corridor "SOMEBODY ANYBODY QUICK HE'S CHOKING HURRY QUIIICK"! Unbeknownst to him, I had composed myself shortly after the splutter, as the volume of my speech was still at its most pathetic, I couldn't get his attention to calm him down, this gave me enough time to enjoy him flapping. By the time he turned to look at me, I was just sat there grinning, poor bloke, he had no idea that this was a regular occurrence, he left quite soon after this, the whole visit couldn't have been any more than a few minutes, it must have shaken him quite a bit.

Things got dark and very lonely at this place. Family could see C.G for what it was, I knew nothing of this – according to my family nothing was ever anything but hunky-dory, they kept any/all negativity/honest opinions away from me to avoid stressing me out. Whilst here, dad was fighting yet more people, authorities, and organisations to get me into the best rehab' he could find. Dad always consulted me regarding "next steps," but I couldn't contribute anything helpful. Alfie was my only concern, so I only said that "I didn't want to move far from him." Of course, Dad came through, he'd found one just an hour or so, down the road in Wiltshire, at the time this one was the most prestigious in the south.

Rehab' number 2 GM. another ambulance journey, it was over an hour but, this journey felt like 10 minutes, after hearing the excitable talk amongst family, I'd filled in all the blanks – "this next place was going to get me back on my feet."

As soon as I arrived, before the dust even had a chance to settle, the relevant professional came to my room to measure me up. One of their priorities was to equip me with splints for my hands and feet, they were so proactive and clearly just as efficient. This place felt good, morale amongst family seriously picked up, almost immediately, everyone was more confident than ever, not that I thought any of this on my own but, feeding off the energy in the room, the dream of getting me back on my feet could and would become a reality here, everything just felt right. It took a few days to get my timetable sorted, before I could get stuck in.

My family loved this place, it was a totally clinical environment, just how you'd want the place tasked with such a feat, to look. My room had its own bathroom, its own hoist fixed to the ceiling – nowhere had ever been this prepared for my physical state, all the staff were wearing uniforms - it just felt more professional. This was where my brain was going to make the most recovery. I would be here for 22 months all together - in that time I would start retaining information (although incredibly temperamental), I would actually start to form my own opinions again, I would manage to make a dent in rebuilding my understanding of "people skills", and most importantly of all, my sense of humour began coming back to me – anyone who's ever met me, knows that I'm a crowd pleaser, a real barrel of laughs, although still immensely intermittent, on the occasions I recognised this coming back to me, it felt amazing, a very welcome, much needed reminder of who I used to be.

None of the staff could believe a 24-year-old was in residence, their typical patients were always much older folk. I was a similar age to a lot of the HCA's so, I got on well with everyone. Occasionally they would spend their breaks in my room, just sitting with me having a chat.

I unintentionally proved to staff that; my mental state was not "well" whilst settling in. For the first few days whilst getting acquainted with different staff, I was often asked my age to which I would always reply with the upmost, genuine sincerity "I'm 21", I gave this answer to everyone that asked, I was actually 24 at the time.

Word got back to Garaint - the manager, he came and explained to me that I'd been giving people the wrong answer, before showing me relevant documents, proving my actual age. I paused, then just burst out laughing, I didn't find it at all funny, I just didn't know how else to react – I felt like a right pirck! The laughingstock, that everyone would be mocking me, 'what a moron'. After being made to feel so positive about everything this was just another subtle tap on the shoulder.

Although my brain was obviously still unwell, this is where I started doing better at occasionally remembering, new names or at least recognising faces, the kind of skill that I had been utterly incapable of since waking a couple of years ago. I also noticed whilst here, that I was relying less on others for everyday information like relating time of day to mealtimes, "midday is lunchtime" etc.

I vaguely recall 2 aunties and an uncle making it over from Canada, to visit me at this place. Really sorry no offense, but 'vague' because my memory was at its worst here, during your visit. The distance from "home" meant that the number of unrelated visitors dropped even more, apart from Julian, they were just about non-existent to begin with, family still did their best to make sure I had a visitor as often as possible.

During the 1st half of my time here, brother Alfie invited me to visit his house, he lived on the Somerset levels then. Quite some time had passed since I last saw little Alf so, I wanted to get him there too, the invite was accepted.

It was a long journey and doing it in that ropey little WAV (wheelchair accessible vehicle) that Alfie had acquired, made it take so much longer but, the idea of getting to see my boy, in a familiar setting helped me 'push' through the journey. This trip took much longer than it should of, I had to get my brother to keep pulling over to "give me a minute." Eventually, we arrived, and it felt just as nice as it did odd, to be in such familiar surroundings. I was pushed into the house and bumped into my friend Meg. For one reason or another, we had lost touch since the first rehab, Meg's house was about a 30-minute drive from my brothers, and way beyond walking distance from even the nearest bus stop, so this absolutely, pickled my brain. I just could not believe that she 'happened' to be there at the same time as me? Obviously, this would have been planned, my brain just couldn't see that.

Little Alf turned up soon after my arrival, this was the first-time I'd seen Alf 'out'. In my head, I'd always thought it would have been different outside the "confines of an institute" but upsettingly, it was the same - I still couldn't chase him, play with him or get involved physically.

"Oh so, this whole needing a wheelchair thing follows me…"

Back at the rehab, maybe days, a week, 2 months, the following morning, I've no idea, Meg unexpectedly strolls through my bedroom door we spent the next handful of hours chatting about anything and everything, as if we hadn't spoken for years. I'd totally forgotten about the encounter at my brothers, I'm sure this visit would have probably been planned then but, I'd slept since then so, had forgotten.

Meg's mum 'Ali' gave her a lift on this occasion, this is where my friendship with Ali began. From this point onwards Meg would visit every single week. Sophie, who I'd known for about the same length of time, gave her a lift, these two became my most/only consistent, unrelated visitors.

While at GM, that pain in my gut that began in the nursing home had been and gone several times. At its worst, painfully, severe sickness would take over for the best part of a week, it was crippling, I wouldn't bring up anything but this thick green fluid (bile), as the retching got heavier and more strenuous, a red tint would become clear (blood), I couldn't eat or drink so, would become "dangerously dehydrated". Since first occurring, the "higher ups" had been monitoring this problem and had now decided I needed hospital. I was taken to Salisbury District Hospital for further investigation. After reading my paperwork, the Doctor decided I would need to be admitted and that I was going to need both a catheter and cannula. "Without sounding like a wimp," by this point I'd began to dread needles, I didn't have them all that often as all my meds' could be taken orally. "I don't care what anyone says, you can always 'feel it' more, when feeling delicate can't you?" (That's my excuse anyway)

So, there I was psyching myself up, getting ready for the needle. The Docter came over holding the usual small metal dish of relevant bits, he checked one arm, then moved onto the next, this was of no concern, I knew he was just looking for a decent vein, but then he started checking my feet, "ahh feet grim" - but not the first time, "if you must...". He finished examining each of my limbs, before calmly letting me know "I can't find a suitable vein, we're going to have to use an artery" – 'oh no, not again, this didn't go very well at Southmead.' "Well, Mr Sumner, we won't be able to use that one again. You have another artery in your groin that we could use?" I froze, remembering that incredibly sharp pain filled my head with terrifying thoughts of needles and blades in that region.

"Mr Sumner?"

I tried my hardest to talk/reason/borderline plead him out of this idea, (considering the strength of my argument – you know when a toddler tries to argue their way out of bedtime? yeah...). After wasting 15 minutes attempting to talk this Dr out of what he deemed 'necessary' – I gave up, thankfully, it took just a few uncomfortable moments and worked perfectly fine. "Phew."

After a few meds had been delivered, a substantial bag of water was connected to my new cannula, time to get rehydrated. Growing up around father, my vocabulary is somewhat comprehensive, possibly even extensive, perhaps? That being said, I cannot accurately put into words how wonderous the feeling of being rehydrated is. I could feel the friction between the bones in my joints, gradually easing, and muscles loosening as my body absorbed the water.

I'm put on an open ward again with about 15 other beds. A couple of days pass, after lots of checks, samples taken, various scans, and whilst being under constant observation, the cause of the pain and severe sickness was found.

The walls of my intestines were now fused together, this was a result of the impact of the crash followed immediately by years of bedrest. In other words, nothing could get through, this explained why I ate so little and why any slight change in mealtime, diet consistency or volume had such a major effect.

I wasn't aware of the details at the time, I still lacked curiosity, I was sort of kept in the dark anyway. Family suddenly came to visit a lot more often, James and Kristie even came all the way down from Yorkshire, before the op' then again afterwards. Not that I picked up on this at the time. I later found out that the procedure I was about to have, was "potentially dangerous." Everyone ensured I was unaware; they wanted me to be as relaxed as possible.

When I woke after the procedure, once I'd taken a few breaths in and out, the front of my body didn't feel right? The skin felt kind of tight? I got somebody to pull up/down whatever I had covering me, and I was stunned. I could see where they'd cut me open, a long slice running down the centre of my torso, all the way from my breastbone to just below where my waistband would sit. For some reason, this hadn't just been stitched back together, but also fastened with metal staples. I thought this must have looked gory, to my fragile mind this obviously looked incredibly masculine, and I was eager to show my big brother, when he came, he looked, shrugged it off saying "That's nothing Greg." – I should have known to expect that, it was just typical one-upmanship, in the way a big brother treats his younger, oddly it was really nice to have that after years of being treated like a princess.

For the longer stays at S.D.H they have a few wards tucked away, for those who need bedrest, "The Spinal Wards." After surgery this is where they put me. I was here for 3 long, slow, dull, tiresome weeks.

They wanted to monitor me, to see how I was coping before letting me leave.

On the day I finally returned to rehab' two youngish blokes were manning the ambulance, neither of which were wearing paramedics uniforms? They were wearing casual everyday clothing? Whilst chatting with them, I found out they were marines, volunteering whilst on leave. I was seriously taken back, not only were they responsible for helping to protect our country but on their leave, they were running errands for the NHS. Before being dropped off, I made sure they understood how grateful I was, I thanked them profusely, saying what an unbelievable job they do, how thoughtful, generous, and considerate they were. I remember how grateful they appeared to be, they enjoyed hearing that. I believe that understanding this selflessness, would contribute massively to my character reform in about a year or so.

Dad had been worried that the rehab' would shut the door on me like the one in Bristol did, but thankfully this did not happen.

They had several separate buildings on the premises, one of which was a small 20-room bungalow, for folk that weren't going to improve medically. I didn't belong here - they put me here simply because it was the calmest building on the premises. Apart from the staff I was the only conscious body in the building, I was put there for a couple of months, to recover from surgery, until "ready" to get on with rehab.

About halfway through my stay in this bungalow, my "state of mind" had become more hopeless than ever, entirely pessimistic, things had become much more physically painful, settling/resting/being stationary was more difficult than ever, it felt like my skeleton was seizing. That red hot inferno of excited enthusiasm I once had, was just smouldering embers by the time I left that bungalow of the living "brown bread".

By the time I'd made it back over to the rehab', my eagerness/excitement/interest, my overall will, had completely dried up, sessions were now much more demanding and had started taking a heavy toll mentally too, big-time, every session, regardless of day, time, subject, instructor or therapist.

This stage of brain recovery became a double-edged sword. I'd regained enough mental strength to understand more of what was happening in real-time but, this development also meant that I could focus down into "issues" a great deal more too. A head full of these nasty, bitter thoughts that my brain was incapable of thinking through/around/doing anything with so, I would unintentionally dwell, my head was a slow cooker - stewing my twisted, illogical, unreasonable, irrational and near-enough always incorrect ideas and theories.

Even though unhelpful - good that my brain was becoming more active, I suppose? "Every negative, always has a positive".

On an average day, my head was nearly always in a state of terrified panic thinking "What kind of father can't even physically play with his child!" "How can I ever be a competent dad? My body doesn't work!" "Why did I have to survive!" "Why bother?" "What's the point in being here?" I desperately tried to counter these thoughts by doing my best to brim my head with positive things, like surviving that devastating level of injury, the crash, coma, and heart issues…

I would find myself mentally arguing against my own thoughts, trying my hardest to counter all the negatives. I tried my hardest, but it just wasn't possible, forget all the injury and physical pain – this confused, soul-destroying depression was torture on a whole new scale.

During sessions my physio's Pete and Tanya would often feel the need to stop and ask, "you ok Greg? Something wrong?" I'd pretend to snap out of it – like I'd just momentarily drifted-off, I couldn't exactly say "oh sorry I'm just trying to justify existing – gimme a sec".

I only ever got out of bed for physio, 4 sessions a week. Whilst awake between my disorientating sleep pattern, I would spend just about the whole of my time, attempting to apply my bizarre, broken logic to my situation. I needed to be able to blame something, blaming karma was easiest, "what goes around, comes around", 'ahh ok yeah, that makes sense, this is retribution, this is what I get after all the wrong I've done, over the years.'

Despite being incredibly rare, I'd started having, let's call them "good days", when my thoughts were more logical and much clearer, occasionally even constructive. It didn't come to me straight away; it took quite some time for me to recognise these.

Apart from the physio, I saw the dietitian "whose name escapes me right now sorry but thank you for that chocolate you brought me back from your trip to Switzerland with your daughter that time". As with most rehabs, a Dr would call in once a week, the Dr here was called Ashlin, she always called into my room whenever visiting.

"I always thought she did this just to be friendly but looking back, maybe there was another reason…?"

Also, throughout this rehab, I had to see a psychiatrist, Kerry. The moment she'd arrive, before she could even sit down, I'd begin bombarding her with questions, "How are you?" "How's the family?" "How was your journey?" and anything else I could think of just so as not to be the subject of discussion. She appeared to find this amusing, she'd always start by reminding me, "No, no, no Greg, I'm here to see how *you* are". To me, these sessions weren't necessary, in my head –

nobody else had even so much as a clue about my dark, ominous headspace. I've no idea what she thought though, she was always busy writing things down.

In life before the crash, I'd become well experienced in the art of deception, so I found it manageable not to say the wrong thing to/in front of anyone, my mental health wasn't ever a cause for concern, "not that I know of any way" I don't know I did this successfully, thinking about it, I had to see the psychiatrist every other week for nearly 2 years? "Hmmm…"

During the time I spent lying in bed in Salisbury, I remember starting to notice that I was becoming able to make sense of things again, but the "sense" I would come up with was always wrong. It's hard to explain.

For example, whilst regaining the ability to focus and pay attention, enough to reflect on current life. I noticed that I could manage having only 1 wee a day. I knew this was odd but, I wouldn't think to run it by anyone, I would just "make sense" of things myself. I arrived at the conclusion that after being such an intense patient for so long - I had been rewarded with this unique capability. Ok, this was more like "imaginative nonsense," a step or 2 beyond "broken logic" but, it seemed totally valid, and a completely logical explanation to me at the time and was enough to put my troubled mind at ease. Considering my devotion to "being healthy", before the crash, my understanding of the importance behind being hydrated and passing fluid was above average. But at this time, I had no idea, this is an example of the day-to-day, common knowledge, that the blow to the head had made unavailable.

This rehab is where my brain made the most noticeable recovery. The improvement in brain function wasn't always helpful.

Yes, occasionally, I could identify problems on my own, but my brain couldn't think of how to resolve the issue, finding a resolution wouldn't even pop-up in my head as the "next step". For example; I could tell that one of my pillows was making me uncomfortable, but wouldn't think of getting it moved, I would just lay there in discomfort, unintentionally up to the point I was asked, (normally by the nurse on one of the 5 medication rounds of the day) "how do you feel Greg?", I would then let them know, and without even thinking about it they would make the required adjustment, problem solved, "oh… thank you". Whenever somebody totally resolved whatever issue so easily, making the problem that I'd endured for hours seem so minor, I'd feel a right dunce. I would just awkwardly laugh it off, but underneath I would be kicking/beating/pulverising myself.

At least I never felt stupid for long, I'd have forgotten within the next couple of breaths.

The issue that used up a great deal of my very limited head space, was the fact that I had absolutely no sleep pattern, other than 20-30 minutes here and/or there, "seemingly" sporadic throughout the day. This really wound me up. I knew I was only 20-something years old and as far as I was concerned Greg was never anything other than a fit and healthy young man. "So, where's the pattern in my sleep!" This wasn't denial; I just hadn't yet "clicked".

I lacked the brain span to properly understand where I was in life, and that I was the one all the Drs were always saying these scary things about. The fact I'd been so close to death just a couple of years ago and that I was going through some seriously intense rehab' following such a devastating car crash, just never even crossed my mind. That might/will sound inconsiderate, and disrespectful, I'm sorry, it's not meant to at all – I'm just trying to let readers know where my head was at.

For the last few years, I'd always drifted off shortly after a nurse's visit so, obviously the nurse had just given me something, I just couldn't see this at the time. My brain just could not connect those obvious dots - this wound me up like you wouldn't believe.

In my head, I just needed to resist nodding off, simple? 'Sorting this surely won't be a problem'. I tried my damnedest, in my relentless efforts to stay awake I would, make myself deliberately uncomfortable, get staff to leave the window open, make cushions/pillows awkward, leave the TV volume far too loud, combining all 3, as well as any other method I could think of, on their own, simultaneously, mixing the combination, nothing worked! After trying every different way I could think of, to an unhealthy extent over a month or so, my fuse was nearing its end.

A result of not having any sleep pattern, meant I had absolutely no concept of time, I've no doubt this sounds petty, possibly even quite a nice problem to have – "complaining about drifting off". But it's seriously disorientating. One day, after exhausting every available option I could think of, during a visit from the nurse I just came out with it, "why can't I stay awake? Why do I constantly keep falling asleep throughout the day?", the nurse replied, "because you have sleeping-medication every 4 hours." "Oh, my daaays! IDIOT!"

I remember, finally finding the answer to the issue that had plagued my mind for months was an unbelievable feeling. Bloody frustrating, I felt like the end of a bell! I couldn't even make this obvious connection, "numbskull"! Anyway, problem solved at long last. Being able to see where my thought process had failed, was brand-new to me. I think this was the beginning of my brain being able to see "the bigger picture", this was my first glimpse of a light at the end of the tunnel, in my opinion.

So, then I asked him about all the different medications, I received, what they were for, frequency of doses etc. There was Tramadol and Paracetamol for pain, Oramorph was PRN (*pro-re-nata,* when needed). Ibuprofen for pain and inflammation, Lorazepam and/or Flurazepam to sleep, and finally Fluoxetine – "hmm what's that for?", "oh, that's your anti-depressant", "Ey?! I'm on anti-depressants!?" finding out about this last one would be responsible for my irrationality shortly.

Learning of all these different meds made me very unhappy, I was only 20-something, practically still a spring chicken, hearing this list of meds made me feel like a poorly, frail, excuse of a man. "I'm not that sick, am I?" Having what sounded like a reliance on medication really upset me? "I'm meant to be getting better!". This didn't sit well with me at all, after getting over the shock of what I'd learnt that day, the upset turned into severe annoyance.

In the days that followed learning of this, my bitter, angry headspace, developed some curiosity, I started asking "who decides this sort of thing?" This wasn't a question nurses heard regularly, most of the nurses 'claimed' they didn't know the answer.

After asking all the different nurses and frustratingly getting nowhere, just before my frustration got the better of my poorly little brain, a young male nurse one day let me know, "it is not the job of nurses to decide what medication a patient takes. Nurses follow the Doctors instructions, written on the patient's paperwork." Then went on to say, "the patient always has the final say."

"So, I could say no?"

"Yes, that's right, then I would mark down that you refused your medication."

"Ahh ok" - so I did just that.

Different nurses reacted differently upon hearing me say "no thanks." At first, they would go and check with their superiors but after a little while nursing staff became aware of what I was doing, so before preparing doses, nurses started to come and check with me first, to avoid taking the med's out of storage then having to dispose of them.

It'll sound pathetic but, this felt amazing, for the first time in years my word actually meant something, my judgment alone, mattered enough to make a decision. With the state of my memory, I literally struggled to remember the feeling of having control, it had been so long.

But "oh my God!", the consequence of dropping every single one of my painkillers, was the most intense throbbing pain from head to toe, all over, the length of my arms, my ribs, chest, feet, shins, right down to each of the individual knuckles along each of my fingers and toes. With the level of friction between the bones in my joints, it felt like my skeleton was coated in sandpaper. All day every day, the same incessant mind-numbing, grating, throb. I was screaming inside, this was both unrelenting and unimaginably painful, made so much worse as I knew, I could have so easily gotten the issue completely taken care of. All's I'd have to have done is nudge the call bell, that sat inches away from my head, a nurse would've answered in less than 90 seconds, but I wouldn't even consider this an option. I'd been drumming it into my head that "you get out of life what you put in", I'd convinced myself it was all mind over matter. "If you want responsibility that badly your gonna have to prove your commitment and push yaself through this" – in my head, enduring this pain was earning my recovery. In a "did the crime, do the time" kind of way. In my head I had to show that 'someone' how much I wanted my recovery.

The pain was made much worse again by the sleeplessness. After spending the last few years being sedated 5 times a day, every day, I found that I was now completely dependent on those meds. For the first few days I didn't sleep once, I didn't even really feel tired to be honest. Of course, I could have asked for medication but "no pain - no gain", in my head it was perfectly reasonable to assume that this self-punishment, would be taken into account by whoever it was deciding my fate, I was desperate to "do my bit". Despite how this might sound, it's not that I was being a control freak, but as this was the extent of my available 'control', I well and truly, fully committed my entire being. In my poorly little mind, I thought "if I satisfy all those sayings in my head (no pain no gain, etc) then all this sickness would be taken away."

But for the first 2 or 3 months, the most immediate issue with living, came along with understanding that I had also built a dependence on those antidepressants too. There and then, I didn't think I missed these 'that much', I'm not sure that staff would say the same. I couldn't see this at the time but, after dropping all those meds' – my mind could manage, much 'deeper thinking,' this generated so many more problems as well as questions, but at the time I thought I was doing ok, maybe I just couldn't think deep enough for the questions to 'bring me down'? I don't know, it's hard to make sense of. All the mental pain, agony and distress is going to catch up with me in a few weeks.

Eventually, the superiors learnt of what I was doing and that I 'appeared' to be managing, as I never shared anything about the 24/7, splintering pain, they then labelled all the meds on my card "PRN".

Another month or so had passed, I found the pain had become a great-deal more manageable, although very much still there, coping became easier, I think I just sort of got used to it? A result of this was that my mental clarity noticeably picked-up, nothing at all substantial but little things like, knowing which day it was, recalling discussions/sessions from previous days, or I might have seen the time and realised "oh so-and-so will be here soon", this sort of thing was still miraculous, but I started noticing it happening more as time went on. Tiny steps like this felt like massive leaps.

A normal day would start in the very small hours of the morning, there was never an expected time for me to 'stir', in these early days – I would only sleep once every 2 or 3 days, even then getting any more than half an hour would be wonderous.

After being off the meds for 'some time', my tv habits made a noticeable change. When I first arrived, I mainly watched back-to-back kid's films, my boxset of "Ice Age" was a favourite, I didn't think much of it at the time – they were just entertaining and easy to watch.

My weekdays revolved around what was on tv. Even though I'd already been awake for hours, for me a day would start when BBC News changed from the overnight stuff to the current day's morning show at 6am, I would then watch "Homes under the Hammer". I knew it was late morning when the double-bill of "Fraiser" came on, I didn't always get the humour, it just seemed like a mature, adult program to watch. Then embarrassingly, I developed a passion for "Bargain Hunt", well, being honest, my passion was more so for David Dickinson – what a guy! I rarely went a weekday without being thoroughly intrigued and mildly fascinated by the characters and predicaments on "Jeremy Kyle", then multiple episodes of "Come dine with me" taking me well into the afternoon, after these I would just watch any old rubbish, more so just staring towards a moving picture, days of tv would be broken up with showers – 3 times a week, daily sessions Mon-Fri, and visitors. Weekends were just hours of "Broken Bad". I swear, I watched each episode about 10 times, I found it so interesting, but mentally, I had great difficulty making the storyline flow, I would focus all my available brain power on this until evening tv began.

Since regaining the ability to reflect, whenever alone with my thoughts, I would often be desperately trying to make sense of my survival. After getting nowhere in terms of "making sense" of the events aftermath, I would always end up feeling an unimaginable sense of debt. I could not get my head round the fact that I was the one to survive? I felt so guilty, I needed to do or give something, anything, I needed to be taxed, punished or in some way penalised. I spent a great deal of emotional energy on this issue.

Joelle – one of the activities coordinators, came to see me in my room one day. After she'd gotten the above out of me, she came up with an idea for me to sort of "give a bit back". She found this charity, their tagline was, "Young people willing to use their past to fix the future, motivated by personal experience to make positive change for themselves and those around them."

"Nail on the head!" Emails went back and forth, before it was decided I would meet with them after completing my rehabilitation. "Amazing", not only did this give my determination a decent boost but, I found that having something (that felt realistically achievable) to work towards, gave my whole outlook/frame of mind structure.

Whilst in bed, my chosen position would be to have the support raised under my head and then beneath my knees (head for comfort, under the knees to stop me sliding down the bed). I would be in this position for 95% of each week, unknowingly enabling the tendons running down the back of my legs to shorten.

I was feeling good, I felt things were heading in the right direction, so I rewarded myself with a new pair of my favourite designer trainers, they arrived, and I wanted to try them on. Whilst someone was applying pressure to get these trainers onto my feet, I found it very uncomfortable, I had never felt this particular feeling before? It was like there was something in the way, of them going on? Naturally I questioned the size – nope size 7 (perfectly normal size for an adult man, just a bit niche). I then assumed the scrunched-up paper hadn't been removed; I was assured that the trainers were completely empty. It took me much longer than it should of, before I realised that the blockage was my toes, they had curled a disgusting amount, enough so as to prevent me getting them on, this was the result of my tendons shortening. "This was the most horrifying of all the reality checks".

Following a standard night of no sleep, mostly spent laid there staring at the ceiling waiting for the 6 o'clock news. Whilst busying my head intensely dissecting and overthinking absolutely anything that crossed my mind as best I could, there was a very rare occurrence, my thoughts were actually relevant.

My disgusting toes were the subject of my thoughts, desperately trying to think of a resolution. After dwelling on this, a brainwave; something truly extraordinary for me at that point in time; "ahh, I need to find a way of stretching and hopefully therefore lengthening my tendons."

I thought, "I should straighten the angles of my bed frame, that'll do it," to begin with this wasn't possible, the process of getting the bed totally flat was very slow, difficult and tremendously painful. If it wasn't for my bitter rage, over Greg Sumner's now pitiful existence, there is no way I could have endured this, or would've even considered forcing myself through this excruciating process.

"OK, this was now complete refusal, I had absolutely zero willingness to accept what I understood of my situation. I would have done anything to escape reality."

Throughout life up to this point I'd always held in/hidden any sort of emotion. But, for the duration of achieving the above, "oh my days" I'd be bawling my eyes out between visitors, sessions, meals, whenever alone with my poisonous thoughts. Devastating upset became the norm, although the pain was substantial, I was crying over my situation. I felt so hopeless, the feeling of doom, over my inevitably sad, miserable future, was crushing. On the bad days I would be pleading to meet my maker, other days were mildly better/just weren't as severe, on these days I would just question if meeting my maker would resolve the mess, I'd made for myself?

Weeks of this pain had passed, and I'd managed to get the bed completely flat, "finally, now my new trainers will fit!" We tried them again and they did go on further, but still not enough. The fact they went on a little further, simply meant my still curly toes could be forced further into the trainer. The further in - the tighter the squeeze. "Hmmm"

Those foot splints, I thought were needless. I'd found a way of utilising them, "wearing them fully fastened, with 'something' under my toes would be a stretch on my hammy's." The something under my toes to exaggerate the stretch.

I implemented these with the same ferocity that I had for my "reliance on medication". In my head "if it's painful, it must be doing something", so I made these hurt as much as I could. To begin with, I could only fold a sock in half (this was the 'something') and stay strapped up for about 5 minutes – before the pain became too much. Throughout this process, I worked up to wearing the splints fastened as tight as possible with the fattest sock I had, fully rolled from end to end, under my toes – for most of the day, the sock was the killer!

Again, I was desperate to show that "someone", who I thought was watching, just how committed I was. I appreciate "complaining" about the strain under my toes sounds pathetic but honestly – at the time to me, it was eye-watering. After a couple of months of this, I got my trainers on, "more progress. Right c'mon, what's next?".

My head had continued to improve, nowhere near being "well", when you're a patient in rehabilitation you're never involved in anything mentally testing. I could hold an in-depth conversation about my life before the crash. But my memory of everything since was "patchy" - putting it mildly.

Quite some time later - in physio one day, I was put into a new piece of machinery which, through various straps, bars, pads and pulleys, would get me into an upright standing position. I thought that all the pain I'd been putting myself through with the splints was substantial but, being mechanically forced into an upright standing position, after being bedridden for nearly half a decade, was almost too much. It was the closest to unbearable, rehab' had ever been but, in my unwell mind 'pain means progress' - so I forced myself through it, "if this was the price to get back on my feet – so be it". The session ended, I was taken back to my room and put to bed, my muscles, tendons, my whole body, everything was fizzing. On that day, I wore my pain with pride, it felt good, like my recovery was actually getting closer, I had actually been in the upright standing position for the first time since waking from that coma! Ok completely mechanically but even-so, as far as I was concerned this was the greatest leap forward in my recovery so-far. "Finally, my commitment has been recognised, all that pain I've persistently endured, is about to pay off."

The next day I was expecting to do more of the same and I was ready for the pain, still red-raw but, "let's get to it!" As per usual, the relevant staff came, got me out of bed and took me down to the gym, no doubt they would have been able to see, hear and feel my excitement, I was buzzing.

I got to the gym expecting to see the kit ready and waiting but, nothing - I thought 'blimey come on Pete, we've got shid to do'. Instead, Tanya came and sat next to me, and immediately asked what my thoughts were on using a powered wheelchair.

"Ey?" I couldn't understand, I'd been in the standing position yesterday? "That was progress, my rehabilitation's finally starting to pay off, isn't it?" It was then explained to me that my physical input on the machine the previous day had been absolutely zero. "What nothing at all? OK, so what's next then? Where do we go from here?" To which I was told, "sorry Greg, but if there isn't anything for us to work with, there's nothing to build on." This was the most deflating, punishing, emotionally taxing information, I think I'd ever heard.

It was so hard to hear, everything I'd been working so hard on, all the pain I'd willingly been forcing myself to endure, always doing absolutely everything that was ever asked of me, had all been for nothing. I thought that bearing all the pain was progress and that my recovery was picking up momentum, heading in the right direction? But no, my dream of becoming worthy and someone significant to Alfie, getting stuck into a career, family, gaining and passing on a load of helpful, inspirational advice that I'd pick up over the years, crashed and burned around me.

I had to double and triple check that I understood what I'd just been told. Cold, emotionless Greg held it together there-and-then, this wasn't really intentional – I think I just didn't quite understand. In the time it took carers to come and get me and take me back to my room,

I'd made more sense of what I'd just heard, the moment the door closed behind the staff who'd just put me to bed, the penny dropped, the entire world fell out from beneath me. The state of my mental competence and inability to understand amplified the upset so much more, the devastation was overwhelming. My brain went into overdrive, I started answering the questions myself - applying my own very illogical logic to every part of the situation. Not that I could see this at the time, but all the answers I came up with lined up perfectly with my very strong sense of denial. I kept desperately trying to reassure myself "well, at one point they thought I wouldn't even wake up", "I've read things in papers/seen stuff on tv before about doctors being wrong", "my survival contradicted beliefs – I could be that sort of case", ideas of this nature hounded my thoughts for the next few weeks, until my next appointment with Tanya.

Eventually it had gotten to the "next appointment". Tanya started talking to me about wheelchairs. I thought 'are you joking? How could someone in my physical state use a wheelchair? According to what you've said, I wouldn't be able to push the wheels?' – (there and then, only manual wheelchairs popped up in my thoughts)".

I didn't want to be rude by showing how moronic I thought her questions sounded, her assistant Pete (handiest guy I know), we'd become quite chummy. When I made him aware of just how ridiculous, I thought all this sounded, he just gave me a wink whilst grinning and said, "just you wait and see Gregory," this was confusing. I was desperately trying to answer the endless questions that this response provoked, this grew very tiresome, very quickly.

Someone came to get me from my bed a few weeks later, saying the wheelchair guy was there to see me. I was thinking, "Fat lot of good this will do," as-per – I was pushed along in my manual chair to the "physio suite" to meet him, all I saw was what appeared to be an electric wheelchair with what I thought was a headrest.

I learnt, it was an electric wheelchair which they call a power chair, and the surface behind the user's head wasn't just a headrest, this was the chairs' controls. I was told, "the headrest is pressure sensitive, the driver controls the chair, via the headrest, push right to go right, left to go left etc".

I was transferred into the chair. There was a stalk next to my cheek, with a button on the end, nudging this would bring up the "options" menu, on the small monitor fixed at the end of the armrest (my dash). I could navigate through the menu's using the headset. The whole chair tilts back and forth, and could recline, the leg rests could be raised/lowered together or even individually. I completely understood the chair's controls, literally upon being told.

From then on, every day I was out of bed as soon as possible and, right from the moment I got onto the chair, I'd busy myself nipping round, happy to see everyone – I don't know that they can say the same, I may have become a tad irritating. "Pfft, who am I trying to kid, all staff on all floors, now had the pleasure of seeing me at repetitive, frequent, intervals throughout the entire day – lucky devils."

After being totally immobile for so long, being able to move round on my own felt amazing.

As lengthy periods in a wheelchair were still brand new to me at this point, I found the kind of pressure on that little chunk of flesh where my bum used to be, was always definite and substantial.

My cold, pure, concentrated, intense, bitter hatred for the wheelchair was majorly encouraged by the main reason - being in the manual chair meant the feeling of complete and utter helplessness. For my own mental contentment, I had to have someone right next to me for the complete duration of time in the manual chair. Otherwise resolving the simplest of issues, slight adjustments to my position, hands, limbs, dry tears, anything physical just was not possible. That and, not being able to check my surroundings, I hated it.

Imagine your made to sit somewhere new to you, you have no idea where you are, why your there, what's going on, what to expect, or how long you'll have to wait, and communicating with anyone, isn't an option. I was still incapable of making myself heard, unless in anything other than a peaceful, quiet, calm environment, even if I could have – at that time my new unsure, introverted, timid personality was more than enough to stop me even trying. The feeling of mental unease was always guaranteed. The anxiety wouldn't stop multiplying, right up until someone was back by my side, even though this was quite an issue for me, would I say anything? "nahhh".

The powered chair put an end to all the above instantly. The feeling of independence I regained was indescribable. Finally, being able to move on my own, after being bed bound for so long was incredible. I still needed someone to open manual doors for me, but this was the most independence I'd had since waking in 2013. I cannot put into words how amazing this felt.

The chair marked the time to move on to the next stage, and there was now talk of me "going home"? At first the thought of leaving this place wasn't what I wanted. I'd been here for just under 2 years; bearing in mind how many "mates" had kept in touch; I felt that the staff here that had looked after me for so long had become my friends. I felt settled, I didn't want to leave. Dad had a word about "the process" and "the next step." I didn't completely understand, but I reluctantly agreed that my time at Glenside had come to its end. "Time to move on."

Immediately I thought "ahh, Alfie in Weston-Super-Mare, yeah perfect, I can finally start building bridges and start making up for all the time I've not been there", that was my priority, "so that's that, Weston it is". We were then told that "I still had a considerable amount of recovering to do mentally" and that "building a thriving personal life was essential to aid further mental recovery." Someone pointed out that there would be absolutely nothing else for me in Weston. So, between the occasions with Alf, I would be pretty much mentally inactive, "hmm, so not Weston."

"Ok then Cheddar! It's just down the road from Alfie, most of my 'mates' were there too, I could reconnect with them." This idea was appealing at first, after all that was home before the crash. But after "going over" it in my head, I realised what an uncomfortable reminder I would be to all those affected by the crash. I eventually talked/reasoned myself out of the idea.

Then someone suggested Bristol, "nah to far from Alfie," then my brother interrupted, "driving from Bristol to Weston along the M5, takes the same sort of time as Cheddar to Weston," well, as long as the journey to Alf is no issue, and there would be much more for me to do with Alfie in Bristol I suppose. "OK Bristol it is."

So, a location had been decided, my automatic instinct was to get online and start looking for a property to rent, the excitement was building, "finally I was going to be somewhere of my own". My excitement quadrupled when I was reminded of the whole journey, surviving the crash, coma, heart, health troubles, attending 2 separate rehabs', a nursing home, hours of operations between 3 different hospitals, it began feeling like my efforts were about to be rewarded, "time to get back to living life!"

A day or two passed – giving my imagination plenty of time to get carried away, thinking of the next stage. Dad and Jen were visiting and the moment they got through my door I started bombarding them, sharing all my thoughts and ideas "woah woah woah not quite Greg", it was then explained that I wasn't yet at that point of my recovery, I needed somewhere that would help me phase back into "life", this would become nursing home number 2. This obviously wasn't welcome news to me; I got quite upset – "seriously? C'mon! of course I'm ready!" (maybe slightly more enthusiastically)

Dad and Jen know me and know what would appeal to me, the nursing home they found was brand new, on a brand-new estate. This was BG, it was at the South Glos' end of Bristol, minutes away from the M5, so getting to and from Alfie would be perfectly manageable. Dad showed me photographs on the website and it all looked great; well, it was brand new, so everything was clean, fresh, smart and tidy "perfect".

Yet another ambulance journey there, I had made this exact journey before, but this time I felt it took much longer; I should have been excited? I was moving onto the next stage of my "recovery", but I wasn't? I'm not sure why, maybe because I'd made so much of my mental recovery at the last rehab, in my mind that place was significant to me? I'd built friendships with the staff, leaving them wiped out a fair bit of my excitement.

I arrived, was unloaded from the ambulance, outside the new 3 story building, and led inside. As I'd found before, the staff were taken back initially, presumably because of my age? No doubt It was odd for them, or maybe even a nice change? As I was a unique case, they weren't sure where to put me? The ground floor was for folk simply of nursing home age. Floors 1+2 were for residents who weren't 100% mentally, Alzheimer's, dementia etc. They put me in a room on the top floor, simply because this floor had the most, spare beds.

This was the first place where I found staff clearly showing remorse for my situation, most staff felt so desperately sorry for me, whenever meeting staff for the first time, a heartfelt apology would come before any introduction, "I'm so sorry, you must be so upset, what a waste of life" – whoever said it, would always do their best sympathetic tone with the face to match, some even looked close to tears. My brain was still foggy, so to begin with I didn't really know how to take it or how to respond. I had a feeling that this kind of introduction was unusual but, as I hadn't ever been spoken to like this before, I didn't understand why they were saying this sort of stuff.

After a short while, my response to these pitiful comments, was something along the lines of, "What is there to be sorry about? I'm alive, aren't I? No need for me to be upset." These words came out so easily, so naturally, this response genuinely surprised me.

One morning, a month or so after moving in, whilst laid in bed staring at the ceiling, during hours of deep thinking, it clicked, "ahh the reason I came up with that response so easily, must be because its true!" A huge sense of accomplishment came with this realisation.

Daytime staff started at 8am, I would have to wait for all the more urgent residents to be seen to first, (on a dementia floor, there was always plenty of these), before staff got round to me. By this time, I'd always already been awake for most of, if not the whole morning. I would be put back to bed before night staff took over at 8pm – mid 20s, living the life of a pensioner, it was ok at the time, I didn't really know any different, and wouldn't realise this for another year or so.

About 9 months into my 18-month stay at BG, I started getting severe pains in my lower back again. Even though this was exactly the same kind of feeling I'd suffered before, my brain was still far from being healthy enough to pick up on this obvious and crucial detail. As my head was still "far from ok", I didn't think of sharing this information. I kept this discomfort to myself for quite some time, it was now pain, all day every day. I mentioned the pain in front of Dad and Jen during one of their visits, Jenny replied instantly, "sounds like kidney stones again," of course! It was so obvious as soon as it was said. I couldn't believe that I hadn't made that connection myself – the pain was identical. This really annoyed me.

This meant another trip to hospital, Southmead once again. I had to have kidney stones removed for the 2nd time. Since my last visit here, Southmead had undergone a major update, both inside and out. After their "update", apart from A+E, wards were no longer open, they were now mostly made up of individual bedrooms. Everything looked much tidier but, being neatly tucked away wasn't so good for me personally, being unable to move, and having such a measly voice, attracting attention when needed just wasn't possible.

Then much to my surprise, unplanned and totally unexpected, Shiffani walks through the door, "Hey $!@£ face, thought you might want some company."

Shiff was a carer from the nursing home, between studying her degree. She had some time off so kindly came to keep me company. We both had the same blunt, dark, non-PC humour, so became good mates very quickly. We spent most of my stay there discussing any old BS. After a day or 2 of aimless chit-chat, Shiff steered conversation towards "getting out, exploring, doing more in/with life", this is where and when the idea of "a life" outside the nursing home was born. I hadn't ever really even considered this a possibility; whenever it did pop up in my head, it was never anything more than one of those "one day…" ideas.

During our talks, every concern I ever mentioned, Shiff would easily counter in her next breath, she actually made it sound possible. After our problem-solving conversation's, the idea started popping up in my head more and more. Understanding this new idea was an actual possibility, meant I began to get bored of my repetitive daily routine. Everyday I'd do the same thing – wake up in the very small hours, stare at the ceiling, whilst awaiting morning staff's shift to begin, then wait a few more hours until they got round to getting me up. Once out of bed, I would always go straight down to the ground floor and just hang around down there, for the day. Visitors dropping by for an hour or so every few days helped to disrupt the tediousness of my sad, dull, boring, repetitive, life. To be honest I had no problem with my life at this point, I didn't yet have the ability to consider that any other perspective even existed.

Although I had been constantly recovering mentally, I still lacked proper brain function. Once Shiff had planted the seed, I started to form an ambition of getting out and "doing a bit", just like most other thoughts, this new sense of ambition, didn't go any further than my own head to begin with.

After spending a month or so problem solving the idea, the concept of exploring seemed doable. Considering where to start, there was a shop just round the corner, that I'd been to with Dad and Jen several times during their visits, I asked the manager of the Care home if I could go on my own. Following an assessment, I got the go ahead, on the basis that I always let the manager herself know each time before I left. This new arrangement felt great, although pathetic, this was my very first taste of independence since the crash, yea getting the power-chair meant moving round the building independently, but now I could go out in public on my own! Life felt good, I was in a nice environment, I still had a few constant weekly visitors and now I had the freedom to go out when I wanted "well, between 8am and 8pm." As pitiful as my life was at 26 years old, I was happy with everything.

I quickly made friends with the staff in the shop (I think)? I was there every day the weather allowed it, constantly finding reasons/excuses to go.

After some time, the short trip over the road to the shop wasn't enough for me, so I started to think about where I could go from there. On one side of the nursing home was this brand new, still unfinished estate, on the other was a much older estate, "explore? Yeah, why not", so off I went along a road onto the older estate, simply because I had never been this way before, so was of greater interest. I'm following this plain, average residential road; I was no more than a couple hundred from BG when I realised that I was uncomfortable. (since having the chair, I had learnt that simply leaning all the way back or forth, often sorted discomfort like this) I knew what had to be done so, I stopped the chair, leant the whole chair forwards, enabling me to lean myself forwards, the plan was then to just sit up again – problem solved. I hadn't realised but, I had stopped to do this whilst travelling down a mild slope, although mild anyone with eyes could see that this footpath was not level, it's not that I couldn't see the problem – I just didn't think to pay attention to the footpath's gradient. There I was, stuck leant forwards (chest on my knees), I didn't' have anywhere near enough strength in my core to sit myself upright, it was already very uncomfortable, and pain was rapidly developing. Then, I noticed a man walking his dog on the other side of the road, I only had the strength to hold my head up for a few seconds at a time – I had to look up, to help carry my voice. Luckily this road was very quiet, I managed to make enough fuss/noise for him to stop and pay attention, every time I managed to look up at him, he was just stood still, staring at me, looking very sheepish, a few moments later he just walked away, "ffs" the pain in my spine was getting worse, "what do I do now!". Thankfully he returned, he had someone with him now, they both started coming my way, the new guy then helped me upright, I rushed back to the home immediately – this incident hit me hard. Another effective reminder of the fragility of my situation. I didn't leave the nursing home for a couple of months.

After getting over/forgetting about that mishap, my ambition to explore was back. As the estate was still being finished, there weren't always drop kerbs where there should have been, and the pavements weren't always finished in places, sometimes, to an impassable degree. I couldn't see this at the time but thinking about it, this maze of hazards was actually very useful, helping to train my mindfulness and exercise my vigilance, in that sense exploring was constructive. I'd always be looking for a new route, a way I hadn't been before, just a street or footpath that I hadn't yet travelled, but inevitably after a couple of months, I'd exhausted the estate, it was no longer enough for me, I was hungry for more. This wasn't a massive estate so nipping back to the home every so often was never more than a 10–15-minute journey – I made sure I did this so as not to raise anyone's concerns as I hadn't yet been permitted to go anywhere other than the shop.

In my head there was no difference between me and any other bloke of similar age, this wasn't me intentionally being mentally strong, this was my poorly brain failing to understand. Exploring the entirety of the estate started to provoke thoughts like "of course a bloke my age, is capable of going further afield" – I often found myself dwelling on this idea, and before long began pushing the boundaries even further, going beyond the agreed route and/or exceeding the agreed time. Sounds funny to say now but, this always resulted in a strong feeling of lawlessness. "Sad 'ey, especially when you take, my life up North into account, but that was where I was at mentally."

Off I went. I'd just turn here, turn there, and see where I ended up. Whilst exploring one day, a little bit further than I would normally, I came to a kind of junction on the footpath, noticing pedestrian signs saying 'MoD'? I realised this must be the big Ministry of Defence building, I'd heard mentioned countless times between staff but, other than recognising its name I knew nothing else.

Even though following the signs for the MoD would take me off the estate completely, I continued, reckless I know! But rest assured, this was no more than a couple hundred metres down the road from the care home.

I was feeling wild, I thought "I'll do a lap of the MoD". I continued following the footpath around the outer fence, running between the MoD's grounds and a very wide, seemingly unused road, (it must have been a weekend – they're closed then) before long a massive roundabout came into view, once I'd gotten to the side of the roundabout, I stopped to take it all in, around what seemed like quite a landmark to me. (I had actually used this roundabout a number of times, it's just a standard 3 lane roundabout, but my eyesight is so poor since the crash, I can't really see anything from a moving vehicle). Adding to my obliviousness my sense of direction was non-existent at this point. I hadn't seen/experienced anything even remotely close to this, the sights, sounds, smells etc since I'd woken from the coma, I enjoyed taking it all in. Embarrassing to admit now but, I remember this little "adventure" was quite exciting.

Anyway, I kept on following the curve of the MoD's fence round to the left. The road to my right was now one of the exits from the roundabout. I came to a drop kerb just before the MoD's security gates, so I crossed the road to continue following the fence, after crossing the road I caught glimpse through a footpath, that cut between 2 buildings, "hmm" so I followed the footpath, to discover a ginormous retail park. (it appeared big at the time - I've been back since and it's not big at all, just a handful of shops with a few different cafes) 'hmm my arms don't work, so I can't do food/drink etc' but there was a huge supermarket. (Again, it seemed huge at the time but it's not even average)

In I went, and I realised I hadn't been in a supermarket for nearly 5 years. Hardly riveting information, I know, but to me at that moment in time this felt significant. Since getting the electric chair I'd become a new man, I'd start a conversation with anyone within range, in my defence I'd just spent recent years of my life being urged to "just ask". I found that a great deal of the other shoppers in that supermarket happened to be of a very kind nature and more than happy to help. Now I could get food (ready meals) here and take them back to the nursing home. This is where I began mastering politely interrupting and requesting strangers help passing me items. When I'd see something that I fancied, I would politely ask someone nearby "excuse me could you pass me one of those please?" They would grab whatever and hold it out between us, waiting for me to grab it, following an awkward pause, using a sort of nodding gesture to indicate my lap area, I would ask them to "just leave/put it there please."

Putting myself in their shoes, I imagine a total stranger drawing your attention to the area below their waist could well be alarming, thankfully I'm still a strong 8 on a bad day, which I think helped.

I started going there often, I got to know some of the staff, well they'd always smile and wave, I thought "oh they remember me," thinking about it – they were probably just being courteous to a customer? Ah well, that's what I thought at the time.

I remember one occasion, there was a female member of staff, judging by her different uniform she was some sort of supervisor, she caught me leaving with a basket on my legs (most effective way to avoid dropping anything whilst travelling), she jokingly (maybe/probably), questioned when I'd return "her basket", I gave her my word, I'd bring it back the next day if she'd let me take it, she agreed.

"Saying this out loud, now sounds beyond ridiculous" – this was the first time since the crash that I had someone relying on me for something/anything, seriously, even if asked my name, whoever wanted/needed to know would always ask the person next to me. Now, I was being trusted and had the opportunity of sticking to my word and returning it the following day. It was only a basket; the supermarket wouldn't ever have even noticed, if I'd have returned it or not. But to me, I'd already gotten a degree of independence back, being permitted to leave the home, (yes, I know I'm abusing that new trust, never mind, greater good and all that – just keep reading) now I was being trusted to stick to my word, this felt important to me. When I woke the next morning, for the first time in years, I had somewhere to be. I'd given my word, and I was going to stick to it. Decent, courageous, heroic, valiant? "Ahh c'mon guys, new man now aren't I"

Then after some time, exploring these areas got boring too. I'd made friends with Tammy who worked at the nursing home, (anyone who thinks that I might have nicknamed her tampon – that's unbelievably immature, grow-up) sometimes on her days off, with the authorisation of the home's manager, we'd get the bus into town, we didn't go for any specific reason, it was just something to do to kill time, at first everything about this trip was new to me and excited my poorly little mind, it felt amazing just to be somewhere different, having spent the majority of recent years, restricted to the confines of a single building.

Tammy wasn't always available when I wanted to go into town, so I would be "creative with the truth", or at least just give as little detail as possible, then hope no one pushed for any more information. When anyone asked where I was going. I'd say something like, "**we're** going into town". This was the start of going to town on my own.

Before now, Tammy had always done all the interaction with the bus driver, so this bit was new for me. I'd get on the bus and indicate/say that I couldn't move my arms to pay, and the driver would just wave me on and say there was nothing to pay. My memory had improved but was still extremely poor, this kept happening, in my head, I thought I was lucky enough to get the same driver every time. I got the impression that I was getting special treatment, and he was being a 'mate', I'd always sort of give a sly nod, 'sly' so as not to let anyone in on our sneaky little arrangement, 'fair play mate' – sort of thing. I started taking different bus routes to and from town simply to waste time, therefore delaying my return, whilst helping to improve on my geography of Bristol and knowledge of bus routes, stops etc. I still believed that I wasn't being charged because I had luckily always gotten the same driver, no matter which bus I used no charge was ever mentioned? I thought "blimey e's a busy bloke".

It's now obvious, what a ridiculous thought this was, but a good example of just how poor my cognitive thinking was then. This was just one of the things that would utterly perplex me on my travels. After racking my limited brain space, I gave up and just told myself that, "if that's not the same guy, it must be a friend of his? Yeah, that's it, he must've told them about me and our little arrangement", this thought was enough of an explanation. I found out a couple of years later it was government policy, disabled people don't pay bus fares.

"Oh…"

It's hard to put into words just how empowering the feeling of getting my independence back was, it was only getting the bus on my own, I'd been doing that since childhood. But I hadn't done anything on my own for years, this made me feel kind of superior, over who? I've no idea - I just felt slick.

The bus ride took about 40 minutes, I would get off at Cabot Circus, Bristol's newest shopping centre at the time, it was here, where I would while away as much of the day as I could. I visited this shopping centre so much that staff in several shops started to recognise me and I'd have little conversations with them in passing.

Meg and Sophie still came to visit every single week. They'd often bring their boyfriends, and we'd all go out for a walk or food something like that, their visits were always a welcomed and much-needed reminder, of life away from being a 26-year-old living in a pensioners nursing home.

Anyway, it's now the spring of 2016. It was a weekday morning, the same as any other, I'd been gotten ready and made my way to the ground floor as Dad and Jen were visiting that morning. My parents arrived and we were sat, chatting in the visitor's area as per usual. Whilst there, the deputy manager of the home came over. In just a couple of sentences she made us all aware that as far as the "deciding authority" was concerned this nursing home could "no longer accommodate me and it was time to start considering my next move", I began explaining, "but I'm happy living here, the staff here are the people I see daily, I even see some staff outside of their work hours, this is home to me", I resisted this news as best I could, it was no use, I was reminded "it has already been decided". This news obviously didn't sit well with me, I could feel the anger inside of me building, the feeling was quickly developing into rage, I'm no longer listening, I was mentally going through the sequence of my explosion, it was just moments away - this was a feeling I knew all too well - here it comes!

The Greg that I'd always known was the sort of character who wouldn't back down from confrontation, if he ever had something to say – he would say it, regardless of who was in front of him. Then much to my amazement, I very calmly just turn my chair around and took myself away from the situation, before my mouth said anything, completely avoiding the explosion. This downright shocked me, genuinely, I had to have a few moments of reflection on this new-found maturity, "Well, wasn't that very grown-up of me!" I was truly blown away, never in my life, had I been so grown up, responsible and dignified.

Up until now I had only ever been "old Greg," the same humour, vocabulary, attitude everything. This was my first ever experience of "new Greg".

In the following weeks dad managed to "talk me round". I did vaguely recall, when leaving the last rehab, it being mentioned that "I needed 1 more residence between rehab and getting a place of my own". Right, so now I wanted to move into my own place, but before I could make that move, the Court of Protection's restrictions that had been in place since just after the crash required me to undergo further neurorehabilitation. (that's what I was told anyway)

At the time, I felt I was perfectly fine mentally, in my head I thought, "this'll be a waste of time. If I wasn't all-there upstairs, I wouldn't be able to get the bus to and from town completely by myself." "Yeah, I think that comment says it all…"

I had no choice, I was very unhappy about this "surprise" additional link in the chain, I didn't want to go through another institution but, after it being explained to me as the most logical and constructive next step, "c'mon then, let's get on with it". To make this next step easier, dad helped me make a list of preferences i.e. location, must-haves etc. I'm pretty sure that I tried to make my hoops as difficult as I could to be jumped through, despite this, yet again my parents had gone over and above and ticked off every single "preference" and found rehab number 3.

This next rehab' was much closer to Bristol city centre. I had my own studio flat here; it was great to have my own space for the first time in so long. Despite my actual life at this point, it gave my self-esteem a considerable boost, which lifted my general outlook and frame of mind completely.

Since I'd been living "down south", anytime I heard any mention of Bristol, it was always something positive, beneficial, entertaining, in some way advantageous. Everyone seemed to aspire towards living, working, socialising in the city, reminding myself of the fact that I had "made it" to Bristol, helped fuel optimism (obviously leaving out anything to do with how I'd ended up where I was). There was only 1 door between me and the rehab', 3 other residents and a whole team of "support workers", so not exactly anything to celebrate, but it did help. This would be where I'd manage to start getting the hang of seeing life from a different point of view – I'd have to.

Since that moment of maturity, when handling that deputy turfing me out of the last place, my eyes had been opened to seeing situations from different perspectives. Baring that in mind, with some encouragement, I chose to see this as progress. It was a grotty little studio flat at the not-so-nice end of Bristol but, as it almost had/did everything I needed, I was encouraged to see it as an ample little pad, a short commute from my son, conveniently close to the city centres amenities. Not that I could see it there and then but adopting this new positive attitude, will not only "get me through" my time here, but applying this mindset will also benefit me countless times in the future.

For the first time ever during my experience of relying on care staff at this place, I found that staff were always busy, on their phones, deep in discussion with each other, on a break, about to do or in the middle of something. None of the staff bothered interacting with the "service users", being heard/listened to happened incredibly rarely. Conversations between themselves always took priority, they did answer call bells, but other than that they wouldn't really allow anything else to interrupt their time. This was the first time I felt such a divide between carers and service users.

The buildings ground floor consisted of, 1 other apartment, the building's kitchen/diner, staff's office, a very small always unused activity room and the living room, and I believe there was 4 bedrooms upstairs, it was a large building, but not massive, (the nursing home I'd just come from had 60 rooms over 3 floors). After arriving, I quickly got bored of the staff and the space. I could easily spend the day with the staff at previous homes/rehabs but, being around these people meant just being present whilst they were having a good chat amongst themselves, the divide was made crystal clear. I decided that I didn't want to be there any longer, 'I'll go explore the area instead.' I asked someone to open the door for me so that I could go out - "No, we don't open the door for service users."

"Ey?" Last week I made it all the way here from the other end of Bristol completely by myself, just to show my face and say hello before moving in, now you're telling me it wouldn't be safe to let me out on my own?

All the freedom, independence, and credibility I thought I'd been building instantly disintegrated, I felt like I'd made/had been making some real progress but, it counted for nothing here. This was frustrating, my blood was simmering, I knew anger was quickly approaching, I started to panic – worrying about an explosive reaction bursting out. "I know I discovered that new-mature-me a little while ago but, I didn't know if he would come through again". I thought, "I need to hide it in front of the staff", being mindful that if I were to fly off the handle, I might have resembled the stereotypical brain injured resident their used to.

"Every problem has a solution"

So, I took myself away from the situation and quickly phoned Dad, I don't want this to read like, "I ran to Daddy" but I didn't have anyone else to turn too, yeah, I've got other family, but no one who was involved in this part of the process and I urgently needed to vent my severely frustrated anger. The next day Dad and Jen happened to be visiting anyway, so I got them to request a chat with the manager on my behalf, I could have done this myself but, coming from a "patient" it just wouldn't quite carry the same weight.

When I talked with the manager, she explained that "as this was a brain injury rehabilitation unit, all the residents were going to say they're fine and they should be let out". After hearing this I thought "yeah ok, fair enough", but it was still upsetting that, everything I'd done for and by myself, all the credibility it felt like I'd built up, meant nothing. Following this conversation with management it was decided that it could and would be permitted for me to come and go as I pleased, only if an OT (Occupational Therapist) agreed that I was competent.

So, before I could be deemed "capable", and granted freedom, I had to be assessed. "Ok, let's get on with it then, where's the OT?" Then I was told "the OT only visits once a week and she's already been this week", great! This meant I had no choice but to wait, surrounded by these staff, in this miserable, dreary, depressing, old building for the best part of a week, "come on Greg chin up, greater good 'n' all that…"

I managed to cope by trying my best to interact with the staff – this wasn't as easy as it sounds, the divide between staff and residents was always so clear, staff made sure residents knew where they were and why they were there.

When there was no one to talk to I would explore the building and grounds as best I could but, as it was a very old building that hadn't been adapted, accessibility was limited.

After a few days, I realised that I'd started to build an understanding of different staff's characters, in terms of their personalities, levels of patience, willingness etc, even kind of figuring out the dynamics between them, when you're a "patient" in neuro-rehab', you can just sit, watch and listen, staff forget you have eyes and ears.

I had no idea I was doing this; it was totally unintentional; I was simply passing time. After realising, I had been doing this without anyone even suspecting – I felt like a real little mastermind, I found this quite enjoyable, in an "I know something you don't know" kind of way, after all, to them I was just another patient.

I soon worked out that the staff seemed to avoid residents, only interacting if they really had to (under instruction from the manager), as she was only part-time – this was a rare occurrence. Whenever another resident was there, (in the most inoffensive, considerate way possible), after attempting conversation – it became clear they were residents in **neuro**-rehab', this seriously limits conversation.

The day of the assessment eventually came, my parents made sure they were there for this. They were just there to back me up, they would've helped me respond effectively, organise my words (if/when need be), at this stage I still struggled to find the right words in stressful/tense situations. As they knew me best – they would know my most likely response/choice of words.

The OT would assess my awareness of cars, drop kerbs, obstacles, foreseeing hazards etc. It was all simple, borderline mind-numbingly obvious stuff. I knew "I just had to get on with ticking the OT's box." The area was a great deal quieter than BG's area in terms of foot traffic. Exit the premises and turn left, this rehab was no more than 5metres from the A4, (one of the main routes between Bristol and Bath) so that road was always busy with traffic, however, turn right out of the premises and that road was a great deal quieter, that's the way we went.

There was a supermarket about 10-minurtes' walk away, this was to be the route of the assessment. I made the journey take about 30 minutes each way, on this occasion. I made sure I let the OT know that I was noticing every single little imperfection along my path of travel, I had to show that I was paying attention and being mindful, when out and about – anyway, I passed.

After that, I was given the go ahead to come and go as and when I wanted. The shop round the corner that we'd visited on the assessment, became my first usual port-of-call. After various interactions with staff and other shoppers, I found this wasn't easy, they were nowhere near as friendly as they'd been in the supermarket at the other end of Bristol, the people around here just seemed different.

Whilst at this place, when down to me - I would divide my time about 70-30 between going out exploring Bristol and my PC, computer time was between getting home and going to bed. On the occasions that weather stopped me from leaving the house, there was nothing else to do other than spend absolutely all my time and attention abusing the wi-fi.

It had been raining for days, I'd been stuck in front of my computer since it began. Through boredom and endless clicking, I accidentally/on-purpose, got to a well-known dating site. I thought "I've been on a couple of dates in my past, might as well make an account, I'm still Greg, I'm still one hell of a catch, they'll be queuing up, if not I'll be no worse off" so, I went ahead and made a profile. But in the days that followed, I wasn't beating them off with a stick? "Odd? Ahh, must be…".

After confirming that the website was actually in perfect working order, I had to consider that maybe my appearance, might have something to do with the lack of clicks? To increase my chances, I put a pre-chair picture up as the profile picture, ok, maybe 1 or 2 more amongst the up-to-date ones. "Yes, mildly catfishy I know but, surely it was only going to be a matter of time now." #clickbait

There had been enough "incidents" where I lived, to sort of re-train my sense for honesty, I could now tell (most/some of the time) when someone wasn't being straight with me, I wasn't always right, but I wasn't always wrong either. It became clear that the staff put me at a very low grade in terms of my mental agility. It was as if they didn't even care if their lies even made sense. I really wasn't happy with the setting, staff or service at that rehab'. Adding to this, my brain continued improving, which was unhelpful considering.

My mindfulness and ability to reflect had come back to me more, which on one hand was good, on the other not so. Yes, this did mean my little world opening-up more, but at the same time, I could also see/understand more problems, things that should have been done but hadn't. My ability/inability to read people/situations became quite unhelpful, and very stressful. I had valid concerns but couldn't voice them, through fear of looking/sounding like "a typical resident, just kicking up a fuss". My brain was coming up with many more questions, queries, opinions and beliefs than it could deal with. All the concerns in my head, that I couldn't say out loud resulted in mentally arguing with my own thoughts. From what I was made to believe "it must be me? I'm to blame, it's all my fault". I think, a result of the toxic frustration this generated, was that I started getting seriously angry at myself. This feeling, the mental space it led to, and the whole "us and them" atmosphere at this place, seriously brought me down, always desperately trying to justify being such a demand on those who cared became the most significant obstacle and my most crucial concern here.

From what I could see/hear/feel/gauge, the general mood was always downbeat and quite tense, the manager being part time and staff only ever pretending to bother when she was around, meant that this place was getting more and more inhospitable day by day. I couldn't trust anyone with anything, from help preparing food, down to laundry. I had my own washing machine, but somehow my clothing kept finding its way from my apartment into the facilities laundry, whatever found its way there always came back with a new hole, stain, or defect of some sort. A pair of my denim shorts came back with new and unexplainable bleach stains on them, considering the rules and regs' around "bleach" in neurorehabilitation especially, those stains must have been intentional?

Just like always, I kept my thoughts to myself. I would do anything to get out of there, it was just under 2 and a half miles into town. Getting the bus was the easiest, most time efficient option but, that journey only took 15 minutes, which would defeat my objective of "wasting time". I could make this trip easily in just under an hour, on the wheelchair. I would make this trip every day rain allowed it. I'd leave as early as I could in the morning and would return as late as possible. I would always go the long way, different routes, via random shops, taking my time looking round, talking to anyone I could, random turns here and there – trying to get a bit lost, anything to keep me away from that place. I just hated being there alone with my thoughts, "yes, I was alone with my thoughts when out on my travels but, as there was so much to consider along the way, traffic, drop-kerbs, route etc, this helped to distract me from the issues and the resulting thoughts".

I'll never forget how one of the seniors made me feel when I was trying to relay a personal issue, he was a tad smarter, actually he was just more cunning than other staff. The reason I say that is, he had a way of catching me out/tripping me up/confusing me with my own words. He was acting as if my speech was so bad, he couldn't quite make out what I was saying. He kept suddenly interrupting and would counter everything "but this", "maybe that" or he would keep finishing my sentence, confusing me and turning whatever I was trying to say into complete non-sense, it wouldn't have taken a boffin to puzzle someone in my mental state at that point but, I say he was more cunning because of how he would disguise this as "trying to be helpful", he knew exactly what he was doing, he enjoyed doing it, and he found it entertaining, as did other staff when I overheard him telling them.

I had a decent "working relationship" with a couple of guys there, but one of them mostly worked nights and the other would go out of his way not to ever let our compatibility show in front of his colleagues. When there was any sort of "situation" they always stuck together, regardless of who was at fault. Every single employee there, were completely different people on their own, often pretty sound and always much more competent, than they would show in front of other staff. Occasionally I would get one of them to come into town with me to feed me, the company of another human was a nice change, we'd find somewhere to eat. It was strict policy that they couldn't ever accept anything from service users but, I felt it was only fair to buy them something, they were only there because they knew I would get them food. Upon returning to the rehab' once together with other staff again, it would be back to normal. Even though this became obvious, I never said anything, I dealt with this by reminding/convincing myself of all the positives of recent years.

This rehab' was getting too much for me, I devoted all my time, effort, and energy to finding absolutely anything to busy myself with away from this place. Being there and needing to rely on those staff felt like I was asking a lot, most of the time too much. I don't know why but here, staff chose to share problems with me, about the facility, other residents, the job, fellow staff, management and even their own personal issues. My own overactive, chaotic, troubled, confusing state of mind was preferable, it was just easier to be alone. Sad? Selfish? Inconsiderate? Maybe, but "please, just let me deal with my own broken headspace first".

This new desire to be alone, wasn't and hadn't ever been me, in the slightest. I've always been unconditionally outgoing, a people person through and through, the centre of attention kind of guy. But at this point I just felt mentally drained, in a weird way this made me feel physically exhausted at the same time. I didn't want to be around the staff, but at the same time I literally could not survive without them, it was torture.

By this point my only regular visitors were my parents. Anna-Marie and Alfie both had businesses to run so, I didn't ask or expect of them. Yes, it had been this way for a couple of years but, as I'd always had mates in the staff around me, time between their visits was heavily diluted.

Whilst out roaming round Bristol, just how few genuine friends I seemed to have anymore, was my next biggest issue. Unhelpfully, my mind tied this in with all the problems I'd spent the last 9 months self-diagnosing and obsessing over, "this must be me too, something else

I've managed to ruin". My head had gotten better but still wasn't at all 'well', blaming myself fitted together perfectly.

It was now the spring of 2017; the weather had started warming up, summer was just around the corner. That dating account had been active for quite some time I had been checking it daily, "not in a sad way honest" but nothing, it was totally inactive, my optimism had fizzled out ages ago, it had become something just to help waste time.

Then one evening…

"Hey, how are you?"

Some "pretty little thing", I wondered if it was genuine at first (since the wheelchair I've had messages from several insanely attractive girls, they are only ever accounts posing as). I came back with something generic like.

"Hey, fine thanks, you?"

I know "Casanova" over 'ere! I needed to be careful, not to sound/react like a bloke who's had a total of zero romantic interactions for the best part of a decade!

We got talking and I discovered that one part of the old Greg was still very much alive and well, Greg's ability to chat-up a pretty girl.

After thoroughly sweeping her off her feet, from behind the screen, I suggested meeting. I wouldn't have ever let her come to me, (a bit scary to say these days but when/if appropriate, I've always tried to be an old-fashioned kind of gent)

"I'll come to you, where do you want to meet?"

"I live in Cardiff"

Ideal, only a short train journey away - I thought.

"No problem, when's good for you?"

We agreed a day on the following weekend. For the 1st time ever in my life, the idea of a date made me sort of nervous, I'd never felt this way about taking a girl out before, "odd"? This rattled me a bit, "how will she react when she hears my speech?" "What if she's embarrassed to be seen with me?" "When she realises how disabled I am, what if she just leaves?". My head was overflowing with worries, concerns and endless "what if's".

The day had finally come, I went and got a haircut 1st thing, then came home and got showered and directed a carer through dolling me up. When it came to me... "ang on, I'm Greg 'FLUKIN' Sumner! Uncomfortable situations? Pfft! Bring it, I dominate situations!" and began reminding myself that, in my opinion - I was actually 'reasonably' well practised – when it comes to "playing the field". Confident as ever – "Come on Greg, you know the drill".

On my way out - phone, watch, squirt of something nice. I'd executed this routine 'once or twice' before the wheelchair, in a way, completing this process again was sort of warming? A welcome reminder of the old days.

Just as I was leaving, an overwhelming feeling took over, settling all my nerves completely, "what's this?" - a familiar feeling but, as I hadn't felt it for so long, it didn't come to me straight away. "Ahh, I remember, my CONFIDENCE! "C'mon Greg, you don't feel even slightly uneasy about treating this lucky young lady, shell be loving it."

"Right, let's go"

I headed for "Temple Meads" station and boarded the train to Cardiff. When you get out of the station in Wales's capital, your pretty much already in the centre. I located and introduced myself to my date, she replied immediately "I can't be too late; I've got to get back." Pretty sure she was just setting up an escape, in case she found me to be a miserable bore and wanted to blow me out, for the first hour of the date, she kept reminding me that she "had to get back", the reminders got fewer and father between, before stopping altogether, "obviously."

We had a wander/roll round Cardiff until the early evening. Me being me, I made sure that we ended up in 'Cardiff Bay', (one of Cardiff's classier spots) I suggested getting a drink in one of the bars/restaurants within the bay, (pretending it was an unintentional choice, but I knew this place was one of the better ones) she agreed, we entered and were shown to a table, she took a seat (I had my own).

When I first meet people, they don't automatically assume that my arms don't work, doing my best not to let me/my circumstances become an obstacle for anybody else, it's not something I announce. So, she had no idea, I suggested ordering her a drink. She kindly replied, "what about you?" I let her know, "Well the thing is, I can't do it myself and I feel it's unfair asking you to." She interrupted, protesting saying "Oh, no no no - of course I don't mind, I'm happy to". I don't know why but, I'd always rather accept an offer, as opposed to ask.

Yea okay, you're probably thinking "well, you should have done that before suggesting ordering drinks, she probably felt that she had to say yes". Ok, fair enough but, as it was my very first date since the wheelchair, I just hadn't thought that far ahead. This situation did help me gauge willingness though, I read from her reaction to the drink dilemma, as to whether I should suggest a meal too, if I didn't see and feel such enthusiastic willingness, then I would of discreetly, made adjustments to the scenario.

It was certainly one of, if not **the** nicest of the restaurants in Cardiff Bay. The mood was just right, we were in a really nice spot, the evening weather was just right, conversation was flowing, we were both enjoying the evening, things were going great. We stayed there for a couple of hours after we'd eaten. It started to get late, she was clearly more than happy in my company, we sat talking, had several more drinks, before deciding to get a hotel.

I won't go into detail, but that night was the most unbelievable confidence boost, wheelchair bound, effectively paralysed from the shoulders down, and creepy new tone of voice, any physical attributes I ever had were now just a distant memory. Armed with nothing more than my charm, wit and a splash of Sauvage, I'd managed, this was reassurance that I did indeed still have "IT". #romeodone

The following morning, after breakfast we left the hotel, and she insisted on walking me to the train station? As the bloke, I felt it was my job to see her off, that's just how I'd always done it, I tried my best to talk her round, but she wasn't having it. For most of the morning it felt like I was being mothered, not in a lovey-dovey affectionate way, more so in a parental way, this didn't feel right. Whenever we spoke on the phone over the next week or so, it was like she kept talking down to me, in the same way that you simplify your speech for a child. Because of this I let her know that I didn't feel like we should carry "this" on, I didn't see her again.

Once I'd gotten back in the swing of day-to-day life, my reality had me feeling low again, whilst out on my travels, my state of mind would always bring me back to going over "the good old days" and longing for time with friends up north, upsetting myself with thoughts like "I used to be someone up north, have I changed that much?" The mates I have left up there are Adam and my mates from school, if only I could get up there.

After getting the train over to Cardiff on my own, a new idea now plagued my mind, "could I make it up north on the train?" In the months following these thoughts first emerging, my phone was always pinging off throughout the day. Through the occasional glance I understood that the boys up north were planning a bit of a reunion via our WhatsApp group "Thuglife". It was always nice to see the same typical, immature banter we'd always had; this brought back good memories.

Thoughts of "old times" were now in full flow. By this point I couldn't get the fantasy of making a trip up North off my mind. As much as I wanted this, when thinking practically, it remained "too much of an extravagant idea, for little old Greg in the wheelchair". But seeing all the constant excitable chat in the WhatsApp group, was getting to me, the reality of not being able to make it was being made worse by my already downbeat headspace.

I'd been researching the journey for a while; it was only ever something to fantasise about and help kill time.

During days of mindlessly rolling round Bristol, I dreamt up a wishful idea. "Imagine if, I were to stay uninvolved in the WhatsApp chat, whilst paying enough attention to understand the date, time, and location of the planned knees up, then just drop in as if totally unintentional". I couldn't get the vision, of dropping in unannounced out of my head, "yeah, I reckon I could make that work?" Although, it was no more than just an appealing idea, to spend time daydreaming about, imagine making it up there for the 'do' - excitement continued to build.

I'd spent a great deal of time fantasising about the idea, and I would always be problem solving the scenario whilst out roaming, I happily did this so extensively as it successfully and effectively distracted me from the usual upsetting, problematic thoughts. After doing my best to think of all the "what if's", I felt confident that I'd thought of every potential problem, times, waits, navigating stations, platforms, getting on and off the trains, booking assistance, needing a wee, getting stranded - as well as feasible solutions/preventions for each.

This would be my most significant trip since the crash, by a long way. I managed to boost my confidence by reminding myself, "I always get the train to go and see my son Alfie, without any problems ever?" Alf's was only 5 stops on a single train. Chester would take between 3 and 4 hours, it was a couple of hundred miles shared between 3 different trains. I managed to counter this concern by reminding myself "A train journey is nothing I haven't done before, what's the worst that could happen". Being out on my own is nothing new, navigating new locations has never bothered me.

"Getting closerrr...".

Constant reassurance was essential, repeating things like, "a train journey means just being stationary between stops. You're in the chair for hours every day – it'll be easy. C'mon, you've spent more than enough time going over this, of course you could do it", a head bursting full of thoughts of this nature brought me closer again to going ahead with the trip. The idea of this journey generated great concern, nerves in abundance and masses of apprehension, but above all immeasurable excitement. "Could I do this completely on my own?" I was eager to prove myself, not only to those who's opinion mattered to me (not that I let anyone know, they wouldn't have liked the idea), but, more so to myself. I was a 27-year-old bloke; who'd just missed out on the majority of his 20's, my hunger to reintroduce myself socially and get involved again, had completely taken over all my available thought space, since talk of this reunion began. In my head, I had been proving myself, with all little trips here and there, doing my best to monitor time between drinks, wee's, the need for physical help etc. By this point, in my eyes I could make the trip. I was confident but still wary, and very doubtful, I remained uncomfortable enough with the idea, to stay onside with my responsible, rational frame of mind.

There had been a "situation" at the rehab', I don't remember details of which but, the feeling of needing to escape that place had just reached its brim and was now enough of a driving force behind the idea, to push me to ignore my rationality. I decided "right, that's it, I need to get away – I'm going to that shindig". Just a few days later, the time had come, since waking that morning, I'd been led there for hours, repeatedly going over the plan in my head, psyching myself up. I'd had a reasonable night's sleep, both of my preferable carer's were on shift – they got me up, showered and in my chair. I was feeling fresh. "You know that feeling when you're getting ready for an occasion and as you make your way down your mental list of checkpoints – the better you feel? I had that! I hadn't had that feeling for years". Yeah, getting ready for Cardiff was similar, but completely different, that was only a date, going back to my old stomping ground was a major thing for me personally. Since escaping Chester, every time I'd ever returned, I'd always done so, in secrecy.

Whilst getting ready, my head and general mood was slowly taken over by feelings of positivity, optimism, eagerness and confidence but above all, the most overwhelming enthusiasm I'd felt since that pesky coma thing, my morale was up in the clouds, I felt more ready than ever. In my head, I was just like any other bloke going on a lad's weekend away.

I'd always had such a definite, intense, passionate hatred for the way that bitter headspace, could so easily overrule, wipeout, utterly demolish my positivity. I always did my upmost not to ever let those thoughts in, easier said than done at the best of times, but daily issues and the same recurring problems meant, I couldn't ever keep the negativity at bay. For the first time in a long time, all the concerns over the endless troubles I'd had for so long, weren't anywhere even close to being on my mind, I made sure this trip had my full attention. After being gotten ready, I was happy that I looked no less than unquestionably flawless, heading to the front door of my apartment I pass my purposely placed shelf of "things" phone, watch, aftershaves – "off I go".

It was now the summer, so it was a beautiful morning, I roll out the front door, immediately into beaming sunshine, it wasn't hot-hot, it was that cosy morning lukewarm kind of heat. It felt great, everything felt just right. Temple Meads station was about ¾ of the way along the route I take to the city centre every day, this was helpful, as the route was so well rehearsed, I could focus more-so on making it up North, instead of just getting to the station. As I'm making my way to the station, the excitement never stopped multiplying. For the last few years, I was led to and sincerely believed, that a journey of such extravagance would never be possible without carer's next to me. The feeling of finally being in control and doing this on my own felt great.

I'm approaching the turning for Temple-Meads, the actual entrance into the station is about 30metres from the main road, at the top of a mild incline. The pavements either side of the road are paved as opposed to tarmacked, the unforgiving bumps meant that by the time I got to the stations entrance, my sunnies are now in my lap, slowing down would have prevented this but, I wasn't going to allow anything within my power, to delay my journey that day, I was feeling so positive. I had this intense feeling of anxious, eagerness, to remind myself and everyone who's opinion mattered, that I was just as competent and perfectly capable as any other bloke . When ordering my ticket, I found out that there was actually a direct train, I could have played it safe and taken that one but, I was so dead set on proving myself, I didn't want to make it easy.

The journey took 4.5 hours altogether, a little longer than it should of but "c'mon, not bad". With the help of staff, I'd successfully navigated the changes at "Birmingham New Street and Crewe".

The journey up north was free of any major mishaps, a couple of minor incidents regarding navigating platforms, pressing buttons for lifts and doors (one of life's greatest banes, when your arms don't work), and managing to rush from a-to-b within stations. ~~I will never hardly ever~~ only if absolutely essential, would I use my circumstances to put myself before others/push-in when there's a queue – unfortunately this normally always results in being the last one - nobody to open doors, no space left in the lift blah blah blah life goes on. Overall, the journey was enjoyable, I'd made it! I got there much earlier than I needed to, partly because of my fondness of timekeeping, partly being mindful of all the potential mistakes I thought "poor little brain injured Greg" was going to make but, mostly because I was so excited. I was on such a high, that being a good handful of hours early didn't matter in the slightest, it was a really nice summer's day in Chester. I felt great, I'd made it all the way up here for the reunion, honestly, I'd passed cloud 9 ages ago.

I had hours to spare, "might as well explore my old patch" whilst eagerly awaiting the inevitable weekend of thoroughly entertaining, impossibly-immature behaviour from a bunch of irresponsible little boys, hiding behind the appearance of being young men.

The weekend blew me away from start to finish – details of which would be unfair on those present to publish. A great time had by all those there - enough said. It got to Sunday afternoon, the boys walked me to the station – "until next time boys, in a bit".

I genuinely thought that whole excursion was going to sort me out and be of some real long-term mental benefit, helping me "handle" life in that rehab, but it was no more than a very temporary sticky plaster. A couple of weekends with my mate Adam would successfully recreate the same relief from my mental unease, but sharing those occasions with you wouldn't do anything in terms of helping to build on the mature and responsible opinion you undoubtedly already have of me. #donnamcgreggerforever. Either way, it took no more than a couple of weeks, before I found myself back in that same old miserable, self-hypocritical mind-set.

It was now autumn, as it does the days were getting shorter and colder, the weather was constantly deteriorating. Despite this, I was still spending the same amount of time out of the rehab', I'd do anything to keep a gap between that rehab' and myself. I would do my best to stay inside shops or at least under whatever cover I could, anything to delay my return, watching consecutive films in the cinema, getting weekly haircuts, exploring every shop I came to.

I'd started getting pains within the left-hand side of my chest. To begin with it was just little bursts of faint pain a handful of times a week, "strange, I've never felt that pain before? Ahh well, I'm still young, it won't be anything serious, no need to make a fuss". As it was only minor and infrequent, I convinced myself to hold back on paying attention. I did my best to ignore it, not to allow the alarming sensation to become a controlling factor, for as long as I could. Even though it kept getting worse, I would do anything to prevent my now feeble, frail little self, from interfering with my life.

It was now about halfway through December, the pain had gotten much more intense and occurred a great deal more frequently, ignoring the concern now took "some doing".

Early one morning I was woken by a severe and almost continuous slicing, piercing pain, shooting around the left-hand side of my chest, being honest, this was properly frightening "I've never heard of a healthy pain in the heart?" When able to focus between the prolonged bursts of pain, my mind was racing, desperately trying to work out/come up with an explanation behind this pain, these ideas of what it might be became terrifying and kept my mind frantically occupied. I was really panicking, this level of pain felt serious, and the location of the pain amplified my dread, I was scared.

After waiting long enough to realise how constant the pain was, (a few minutes) I called an ambulance "hey Siri", the paramedics on this occasion were 2 young females, they must have been around the same age. This rocked me severely 'they're my age, with their whole lives, and careers in front of them, I would/should be around that stage in my life', this thought well and truly crushed me.

After giving me the once over whilst still in bed, they told me "We can't find the problem with the equipment we have, you need to go to hospital".

Bristol Royal Infirmary (BRI) this time. After hours of nerve-wracking tests, they found 4 hernias, a handful of gall stones, an equal amount of kidney stones, and I had pneumonia again – this "aggressive inflammatory infection" was responsible for those pains in my chest. Where the top of my lung was in contact with my heart, the infection had been passed over. The sharp, shooting pains were caused as bloods flow through my heart was being restricted. "Phew, nothing serious then…"
I've always thought of myself as being physically resilient but, this was

another startling reality check, since waking in 2013. "Is this my life now?" "What about Alfie?" "How am I ever meant to be a dad?" I felt so weak, helpless, and vulnerable, overall, a pathetic excuse of a human. The hospital said, "it would not be safe to let me go, with an infection of such severity", so kept me in for treatment. I couldn't get these haunting thoughts off my mind, "I'm only 27 years old, I'm well and truly doomed, how long do I have left?".

I was put on a strong course of steroids and a couple of other meds. They told me that the hernias, stones in my Gaul bladder and kidneys didn't need any immediate treatment, so I got to keep them.

While at this rehab' I formed a relationship. And I became a father for the second time. Dominic was born on the 25th of December, but sadly my relationship with his mother broke down before his 2nd birthday. All my focus has been on trying to see as much of Dominic as frequently as possible. Being totally physically immobile presents challenges regarding "effective parenting", and when parenting young kids, that list quadruples. Constantly pushing myself to overcome the upset caused by my inadequacies in parenting became the tallest order I had ever faced.

5 more equally, upsetting, tormenting, mentally and emotionally exhausting months passed, before at long last; I now ticked the box of "completing neuro rehab'". I could now move on and start looking for a place of my own, within seconds of hearing this news, my hunt began.

I knew that I didn't want to live anywhere that resembled being in, or even close to the city, this meant searching the "South Gloucestershire" end of Bristol. I was in full control of this project, everything from finding and choosing the property, setting up viewings, getting to and from, having full control over this project felt good, "finally I'm being trusted, finally people/they/someone actually has faith in me".

After arranging a viewing, it would then take me the best part of a day to get ready, i.e. research and memorise the location, which bus to get - where to get on and off, the address in case/for when I'd need to ask someone. Getting to this end of Bristol during the day, took just over an hour, between 2 buses. Regarding navigating new, unfamiliar areas with a dodgy memory, imagine taking directions over the phone, in broken English, from someone who'd only driven through the area a few years ago, "yeah, tricky".

I would find a landmark/point of interest (shop, roundabout etc) near the destination, that I presumed would be well known so when needed, I could ask someone how to find that spot, then remember how to navigate from there, my idea worked perfectly… nearly every time. The fact that I'd managed to overcome this navigation issue, genuinely, surprised me. My ability to problem solve, had clearly made a noticeable improvement, 4 years ago I wasn't even sure of my own age - realising this made me feel great. Yes, making the journey up north was an achievement but, I had the safety net of having the stations staff around me, when needed. Whereas the above, was almost completely down to me. Before I get too carried away biggin' myself up, I should confess, it wasn't until my 3rd attempt that I attended a viewing. "Anyway…"

So far, I'd only found and attempted viewings on apartments, as I was sticking to my budget. After not even managing to attend the first couple of viewings, my patience was running on empty. I felt so close to getting the whole "morbidly ill," phase behind me, getting away from that rehab' and starting the first chapter of my new life.

I kept searching, I found a bungalow in Patchway, slightly above the monthly figure I'd set but, like I said, "running on empty". It was in my chosen area, had 2 bedrooms, plenty of garden for my boys, it was perfect, I went ahead and booked a viewing.

I thought it best to meet Dad there for this viewing, for a few reasons, 1. Over the years I've found that some people just "appear" to be listening to me, they put on their best "I'm listening" face but aren't paying attention. So, I wanted Dad there to help get my words across, if need be.

2. Dad's very good with his words, he would be helpful in securing the place if I decided it was right for me, reason number 3. Considering my track record, there was a good chance that I was going to miss this one too, dad could have done the viewing on my behalf.

I left the rehab' way too early, leaving more than enough time to compensate for all the mistakes I might have made along the way, the plan worked – I was there on time. When I got there, the estate agent was already doing viewings, there was a couple left before it got to our turn. Finally, the couple exited the building as did the agent, before calling us over.

It was a good job I had Dad there because I couldn't even access the building, there was a step at both the front and rear doors! Dad went in to have a look around and assess whether we could "make it work". He came out and confirmed that it could be made suitable, this was exciting, "so, we should let the estate agent know?" We did exactly that there and then, the estate agent replied, "Ok great, I'll put you on the list, as there were others who'd already said that they wanted it". Typical, another one I've missed out on, o'well I'll keep looking - for me that was it. But when I turned to Dad; he gave me that ever-reassuring look, "I'll have a word."

Dad armed with his "silver tongue", went to the agency immediately, he subtly let the staff know of my story, and what I'd been through since the crash, told them I'm quite the advocate for road safety now as a result; and dropped in there about my TV appearances. By the time he'd finished, the staff had put me at the very top of the list of applicants, they even phoned the landlady before Dad left; to personally vouch for me, she agreed to let the house to me. At long last, I'd gotten a place of my own. I got the keys in March 2018; I was settled in by April.

A month or so after settling, I was being woken by pain at least 3 mornings every week. This was worrying, although by now I had experienced quite the array of different pains, I had never felt this needle-sharp pain around this particular location, I had no idea what it was. Not that I knew it yet, but this latest predicament would be incredibly effective help in terms of 'retraining my brain' – and then some…

I have one of those electric adjustable beds at home, and found that by raising both ends, effectively sandwiching myself helped very slightly, it was nothing even close to relieving the pain, but it did help marginally, this along with the maximum doses of the painkillers that I had access to and could mix, did help to ease the pain a little more – not even for very long but, it's all's I could do.

On the most severe occasion, I had been up in excruciating pain for hours, the cause of which was still unknown. It had gotten to early/mid-morning, the level and continuity of the mysterious pain warranted calling 999. When they arrived, all the standard checks were done, heart rate, blood pressure etc. After interpreting the results of the tests, they decided a hospital trip was necessary. Southmead again this time, a few scans later and my curiosity was answered – those kidney stones that B.R.I. found, they were on the move.

The doctors then broke it to me that "this collection of stones could not be removed surgically, "as you have already had the procedure several times Mr Sumner, you will have to wait for nature to take its course." Without hospital's "real deal" intravenous painkillers, over the following 3 or 4months I was going to learn about unmedicated pain. If you've never had traveling kidney stones imagine, shards of broken glass being gradually dragged through your insides, from just below your belly button, down to your genitals.

"Apparently" my kidney stones were not even half a teardrop in size, but it felt like once passed, I could've had some sort of rockery-esk garden feature assembled with them, I was going too – I just felt unfair asking my carer to carry them all the way to the back garden.

Even though I'd developed kidney stones several times since waking from the coma, I still hadn't learnt/retrained my brain to drink regularly – I understood that nothing running through my kidneys meant stones developing, but the moment the topic of conversation changed, this information would instantly shoot to the back of my mind and would only "come back to me" when relevant. A catheter would have been an appropriate solution, but no thank you. Appearance has always been a priority of mine, I wouldn't even consider the idea of being out in public, with a bag of pizz hanging off me. I had always assured myself that, I could still manage to brush up "ok", for me personally, a catheter would simply create another hurdle. Although many would consider the ability to relieve themselves without needing to visit the bathroom a bit of a treat, for me looking good or at least just not looking as unwell as I am, comes first.

It would take months, for the frequent, intermittent periods of piercing, soul-destroying, pain to pass altogether. Once the last of the stones had passed, it felt like enduring the terrifying, confusing, uncertain, instability, of my recovery had actually come to an end? It felt like time to reward myself? "finally!" I could get back to living life. I had some making up to get on with.

Organising my daily life was now completely down to me, things were going well, nothing remotely close to "fine" but satisfactory, for me at the time anyway. Not that I had much of an opinion, although cognitively I had improved a great deal, new/unfamiliar scenarios were still tricky for me. My brain was still not well enough to pick up on details or notice anything that wasn't quite right, for example, even though I now lived in a bungalow and my bedroom is at the front of the house, just a couple of metres from the road - I didn't put curtains up for another 2 years – I just made do with that rubbish netting stuff.

Anyway, the new gaff, is a stone's throw from the M4, even closer to the M5, stops for several different bus routes into town and/or other POIs in the area are no more than a couple of minutes from my door. it's between 2 retail parks, one of which is next-door to Bristol's biggest indoor shopping precinct. Bristol's 2nd most major train station is only ½ a mile away, honestly its ideal.

Getting to this point had been full of tears, upset, a traumatising variety of pain, a shocking amount of frightening, startling, depressing experiences and information alike. Whenever me and family had spoken about getting to this point, it seemed like a fairy tale, it just didn't ever feel possible. But at long last, I could finally get back to living life and piecing together a future.

After the most stressful, emotional, turbulent, demanding, physically and mentally punishing, exhausting years imaginable, everything was finally falling into place. In my still fuzzy brain, I'd gotten to the end of that scary medical phase, I felt like I'd made it out the other side.

I had been living on my own for a couple of years, and getting the hang of almost managing life again, when a random interaction one day got me thinking.

I'd just been to meet my parents at Sparks&Mensors cafe for a coffee (yeah, ghetto I know but that's the sort of cool cat Greg is now) and was now waiting at the bus station. Waiting at the same stop was a mother of similar age, sat with a pushchair - we got talking, we're now having an in-depth talk, I was explaining something about my kids and parental restrictions – due to being under "The Court of Protection", and why I thought the family court mightn't take me seriously, (this sounds as if I flippantly discuss personal things with "anyone", well yes, I do. For the last 8 years, I'd been discussing personal issues with whichever carer happened to be next to me at the time, I'd lost that sense of what to keep to myself, it turns out this is a very difficult habit to lose) I could see genuine disbelief on this person's face, this perked my curiosity. This took over pretty much all of my available thought space for the next few months.

After many mornings led awake reflecting on where I was in life and where I would like to be, it came to me "yeah! My mental capacity has definitely/probably/possibly/maybe improved, I reckon it would've/could've/should've/might've done so enough to be recognised officially and get me out from under the "Court of Protection" and more involved in my boys' lives. Any mental improvement I'd made, wasn't an easy thing for me to notice personally - little things like, thinking of getting a large, dry-wipe calendar, to help with my abysmal memory (large so it's easier to see, drywipe so as to be easy to edit, coming up with this practical, pragmatic solution blew me away a bit, truly a eureka moment.) The fact that I could hold a conversation for longer, without losing track of what I meant, or what I was saying/being told... as much. Despite this new frame of mind becoming apparent, just like always, I kept everything to myself.

Enough time had passed, for the above thoughts to stew. After convincing myself of how far I'd come, I wanted to get my thoughts verified, by the deciding authority, the powers that be, "The Court of Protection". Despite wanting to get the ruling amended so badly, I was still very much "on the fence". I was still confidently, mentally echoing, and unintentionally, stood-by exactly what I'd been hearing for years, regarding the "health of the brain and its ability following such severe injury blah blah blah…."

I don't remember what but, something regarding the can/can nots of the order had gotten in the way of my plans one day, I decided the time had come to see if my mental capacity had recovered enough to change the court's ruling. In my opinion I was now capable of handling life by myself, meaning the practical stuff, finances, contracts, bills. At this point, any kind of responsible decision required the joint approval of my "Powers of Attorney" - dad and a team of solicitors.

I'd worked out that I wanted the above, I just had to find out how to go about it.

Following that conversation at the bus stop some time ago, regarding my boys. I'd found a local law firm, whilst I was there one day, sat in the waiting room, I spotted a leaflet with the title "The Court of Protection," I couldn't pick it up and investigate obviously, so I did my best to make a mental note to investigate this when I got home.

I'd learnt by now, the most successful way of remembering mental notes, was to find a way of relating the note to something practical that would be happening relatively soon, i.e. getting home, my next meal etc. When the "something practical" occurred – this would trigger the memory – this only worked occasionally.

Once I arrived home, the above technique was successful, I got things underway as quickly as I could, before the voices of reason, authority, contradiction - in my head became loud enough to put me off. I found the number for the firms' relevant office, I took a few moments to compose myself, rehearse what to say and summon the courage to make the call. It may sound pathetic, but this had been the most important, significant, critical, seemingly immovable obstacle, since I started piecing my life back together. The Court of protection have the power to put anyone under whatever legal restrictions they feel necessary, the idea of confronting their 'might' was daunting, the fact that I was so heavily reliant on their legal authority, had been so firmly cemented in my mind over the years, I was incredibly unsure, wary, nervous.

I began by asking some questions, simply trying to find out if reaching the desired outcome was even possible. I'd already found the answer online, but you can find your most preferable answer to any question on the internet can't you, I'm not too sure that "some keyboard warriors' opinion" would hold much strength, in terms of legalities.

I was asking everything in the 3rd person, not sure why? In case I was about to sound like an idiot perhaps. I understood that "yes, following a re-test, my mental capacity could indeed be officially reinstated". I went ahead and booked an appointment with the relevant solicitors, not for the actual retest, just to go and discuss options. I never stopped referring to myself in the third person for the entire phone call, "what a douche!" Anyway, I was now another step closer to achieving what I'd always thought of as an unreachable outcome.

A month or so passed and the day of the appointment had arrived – I travelled across Bristol to the office of the solicitors concerned; I was finally sat in a room with the guys who kind of held the key to me regaining my capacity.

Were sat round a table, in my head the atmosphere was tense, to these solicitors - I'm sure it would have been just like any other appointment, but there was a lot riding on this for me. I had been talking for a few minutes explaining the history behind the court's decision. After detailing the ruling that the court of protection had over me, particularly that "on paper" I didn't have my capacity, they felt the need to stop me and double check that I was talking about myself! This made me feel great, internally it was the 5th of November, overjoyed excitement started imploding. My nerves were rebounding off every surface in the room, nowhere even remotely close to being settled. Obviously, Greg Sumner, managed to keep this hidden and maintain his usual cool, calm, composed and entirely collected appearance – "pfft".

The meeting ended, I'd learnt that I could indeed instigate the retest completely on my own, this would require a neuro Dr to evaluate my mental competence, then the results had to be authorised by the court. I went ahead and booked their doctor.

By the time it was approaching the Doctors visit, it was early 2020. There had been covid stories plastered all over the news for months. By this point, it looked like this "covid" was going to be so severe that it might ruin any chance, I ever had of getting the official status of my mental well-being re-recorded.

Being honest, after considering that my body has been rather fragile since the crash and that in terms of health, I was now "vulnerable", I developed a sense of fear, not that I would let anyone know – as they (those who'd cared) had been there for me all the way through; I saw this as a chance to give a bit back. I put so much effort into keeping this fear-driven, anxiety hidden, I thought, sharing anything of my concern would get family fussing. I just didn't want to "make it all about me" again. I helped to keep the concern at bay by distracting myself, I pushed myself to focus all my attention on the appointment with the Dr, trying to think of everything he might have asked, then prepare and mentally rehearse my answers. The lock downs and restrictions didn't impact plans all that much, it did interfere/delay things slightly, but only by a month or so. It was May, between lockdown 1 and 2, by the time the doctor came to carry out the test.

I was expecting, a Dr tasked with such responsibility to be of the upmost formality, but when the Dr arrived, I didn't get that vibe at all. I'm not saying he was a scruff; he was simply more relaxed than I'd imagined. We said our "hellos" - then got on with it.

At the beginning, I found most of the questions he asked seemed simple like, "what is 50% of 100?" Personally, I thought of this as an easy question "is he being serious? Ahh this must be a trick?" My mind was racing, furiously trying to work out if this simple question could provoke a silly answer. He then asked me to explain my workings out too, "workings out? There isn't much to work out – "yeah, this must be a trick question".

Adding to the pressure, math's was by far my worst subject in school, not because I couldn't do it, but because I didn't get on with the teacher, I would purposely get thrown out pretty much before even sitting down at the beginning of a lesson, between doing this and being suspended so much, I missed many maths lessons, this shows today.

I said, "am I allowed to use my phone?" He said "Of course – just verbally explain your workings out". I can only operate my phone using my voice, so I thought, "perfect, two birds with one stone". I could have just repeated the question to my phone, but I thought "I'll make my workings out sound just a little more complex", "hey Siri, divide 100 by 100, then multiply by 50" – hopefully demonstrating that my brain could comprehend and process instructions and questions - come to think of it, I probably just made it look as if my brain was complicating a simple question? Anyway, my intention worked - or at least it didn't backfire. After about an hour of watching this man frantically scribble down notes following each answer I gave, he very calmly just said "ok you've passed."

I was thinking 'Oh so that's it? Surely not?' I asked him "all the restrictions lifted just like that?"

"Yes. I will submit the paperwork, and you will receive your certificate in a couple of weeks. Bye."

Wow this meant, that I was now deemed a normal functioning member of society again (yea not entirely but, on paper). I was hesitantly over the moon.

A few weeks brimmed full of tormenting anticipation passed, whilst awaiting the certificate, finally a letter arrived with a return address of the court on the back. 'This is iiit!'

After opening and reading the first few lines, I understood this wasn't the long-awaited piece of paper that confirmed I'd officially regained my capacity. I read that, although the court had received the Doctors papers, they wanted to send one of their own Doctors to verify the first Doctors findings. "Yeah, it did seem a bit too good to be true." This made me question if I really had made the improvement, I thought I had. The feeling of disappointment started creeping up on me. "Am I not better after all?" this brought me down big time, this was deflation on a whole new scale but, after reminding myself of the new positive Greg, I wasn't disheartened for long "another test? Bring it on."

"If at first you don't succeed, try, try and try again".

It was now about a week before lockdown number 3, I received a call, letting me know to "expect the doctor in 2 days". It was the day of their Drs visit, following a very tense mornings wait it had gotten to mid-day, the Dr arrived. As soon as he entered the house, I immediately got the impression that he was of a more sincere nature, he matched my idea of what to expect perfectly. He didn't even need to say anything, this guy just had a way about him, sort of like a headmaster, a very authoritative kind of manner.

I often use humour to try and gauge a situation, or when meeting someone new. I tried lightening the apparent atmosphere "sorry, I would shake your hand, but…" and shrugged, sort of gesturing that I cannot lift my arms, usually this would at least provoke a "oh, don't worry", but he wasn't having any of that – he replied, "I wouldn't shake your hand anyway - Covid".

"Oh…."

We got on with the test, and once again, some of the questions seemed almost silly to me, but I was ready to deal with them, having experienced similar last time.

It started to feel like he was deliberately trying to trip me up/confuse me, considering my mental fragility since the crash – he very nearly managed. It wasn't that his questions were any more testing, it was the way he worded them. They became questions within a puzzle of words, which did take me longer to work out.

I was so scared that he was going to show me up, ruining all the progress, I felt like I'd made. I could feel the most intense heat building deep within my chest, this was frustration of the greatest, most volatile toxicity simmering. I knew I was getting angry; he wouldn't have been able to tell, it was upsetting me that he was deliberately trying to trip me up, my frustration was so close to boiling over - I nearly exploded, the old Greg would have lost it ages ago, but the new Greg managed to successfully keep these feelings hidden. The test finally came to an end, I could hear my heart pounding in my ears as I asked him "how have I done", and he said that he was happy to agree with the opinion of the first doctor.

"Wow, I'd done it AGAIN!" I had done exactly what I had thought of as one of those highly unlikely, almost completely improbable "one-day" ideas. My mental capacity had been, getting better over the years. I'd been tested by two specialist doctors, and they had both agreed that I was mentally competent enough to handle my own life again, my whole life had been given back to me in that instance. It felt amazing, I was so happy, but with the Covid pandemic constantly developing, I couldn't exactly go out and celebrate. I did, however, treat myself to a very nice piece of filet steak, for my dinner that night.

"Finally!" This was the closest I had ever been to getting that nasty event of 2012 almost totally behind me. Physically, I haven't really made any improvement, bit of a bummer but, along with amazing parking – it does have plenty of other perks. After taking time to focus and reflect on the whole episode, everything that might've, could've and did go wrong, it came to me "FUUUDGIN 'ELL! I haven't done too bad, have I?" Following this sort of thought path, identifying and focussing on the positives instead of dwelling on the oh so many negatives, made me feel utterly amazing. I felt that mentally, I'd come through it too! It felt like a huge weight had been lifted literally upon being told.

From this point onwards it gradually dawned on me that, I could now do what I wanted, go where I wanted, when I wanted. It had been officially certified that my brain had recovered enough to control everything in my life, finally my word actually meant something again, I had authority over everything in my life, "the buck stops with me!"

These days it's my name on all the post that comes through my door, I'm probably the only person who enjoys getting bills, it's my name on all the paperwork. I recently renewed my eldest son's passport, I did absolutely everything required to get this document completely on my own, the feeling of being able to do "parent stuff" was brand new to me and felt great. It might sound stupid, but these are things I couldn't do before. For the first time since that devastating incident of October 2012, it felt like that door could be closed behind me, and I could carry on with my life. After everything that had gone wrong, everything I'd made it through, the feeling of getting to this point felt incredible.

Chapter 11

The "new Greg" and life today

2020 –

In October of 2012, I was so badly injured that I was unrecognisable to my own brother. On numerous occasions over the following months, my body kept trying and came extremely close to shutting down for good, for the first 6 weeks of the coma, I was within touching distance of "death's door". As the weeks became months, family and friend's fears over not ever seeing, speaking, hearing, holding, joking with their son, brother, cousin, nephew, uncle, friend, that they'd shared their life's with, was a frightening possibility.

It has been the longest, hardest, most straining, stressful, exhausting, punishing, frightening, overall, the toughest, most gruelling episode of my existence. But after spending almost the entirety of my 20's between rehabs, hospitals, and nursing homes my daily life had now found an even keel. By a long way, the best and the worst experience of my life so far.

Look at me now! Not only did I wake up, but I'm now the father of 2 very handsome young men, I live at my own address, I have a life full of the usual routines – food shopping, school runs, paying bills, finding deals when renewing various insurances, paying attention to different forecourt's price per litre.

The "old Greg" could be and often was a very angry, unreasonable, irresponsible, selfish, volatile young man. He was 100% "me, myself and I", he "thought" he took care of himself, and that he didn't need anyone else. He was known to numourous police forces and courts up and down the country, generally, not a very nice individual.

After waking from the coma, it took years for me to fully understand what had happened. Whilst prospects seemed to continuously worsen, I had to take on the reality of my injuries. As I slowly regained my mental strength, my head was full of grave concerns regarding what kind of a future was in front of me, if any at all. Very dark, frightening times, full of worry, and what I believed to be valid concerns. The mixture of having a head full of alarming, unanswerable, frightening thoughts and not being able to come up with sensible, or even logical answers as well as being unable to navigate such headspace scared me.

I felt so alone, so frightened, I felt that my life was over, but I've almost completely made it out the other side. The new Greg is a much happier, more positive and optimistic character.

The old Greg accepted defeat much more willingly, he would jump to and accept thoughts such as, "Well, that's it" "There's nothing else I can do/can be done" "Whatever, who cares anyway" but now I'm in a much better place mentally, when I encounter problems, I no longer focus on what can't be done, instead I will push myself to find a way of making the scenario work, move, gather momentum. I'll say to myself, "Okay, where do we go from here?" "What's next?" "What can I do with this?" A stationary, motionless situation becomes stagnant, this isn't doing anything for anyone. It isn't always easy, of course not, more often than not enduring the rough to get to the smooth is part of the process and will be essential. Managing to adopt this mental approach has helped me through, some of the most intimidating darkness, and overwhelming bitterness imaginable, a truly torturous headspace – thanks to my new mind-set and outlook on life, I've managed to leave just about all the negative parts of the "old Greg" behind me, enabling me to move on.

As the "new Greg", I am a happier, more positive, patient, much more amicable individual in general. I've come through it, and I've become a better person for it. Some of "old Gregs" traits do occasionally interfere but overall, I think I'm doing ok.

> "You can't change life if you don't change something…"

Find, cause, create, your own catalyst, your own "something" that will help generate enthusiasm, use that emotion to encourage your determination, propelling you forwards, through or around your issue, problem, dilemma. It can be done; persistence is key.

I'm still in a wheelchair and unable to move voluntarily below the shoulders. It would be so easy to remain down, depressed and endlessly pessimistic about everything I've lost. Bitterly cold mental darkness, hatred for myself, my situation, the things I can't do with or for my boys, the life, job, career that I was kind of managing to build, life's end goals and aspirations now looking unattainable, memories of my jaw line continuously fading and all the things that my future now won't include, is indeed always there.

I could easily go-on about my problems, issues, incapability's, things that upset me/my life, all the limitations that cause physical, mental and emotional pain, everything that reminds me of the trauma but, I know that wouldn't do anything for me. I have done and still do my upmost not to allow that hopelessly downbeat headspace to exist, after realising that I had the power to do so.

> "Make the most of what you have, it mightn't be there forever"

Although always 'just there', I've managed to find a way of 'handling' this frame of mind, I know if I let that headspace exist it would win. It wasn't easy but, after getting my head round everything I still can do, I realised "life is what **YOU** make it", I've managed to take on a "never say never, go for it" – type of outlook. This opened the door to not seeing obstacles as impassable but, spending energy on finding a way round them.

I've been a father since I was 20 years old, but now I can be a parent, ok I have a few hurdles to negotiate but, "where there's a will – there's a way." I am determined to be the best dad possible to my boys.

That devastating crash stole a considerable chunk of my life. It breaks my heart that I can't be more involved with my boys today. When I was young, I remember looking up to my dad so much, he was the absolute pinnacle of existence. I will endlessly miss being that person to my boys, but instead of wasting time, dwelling on it and upsetting myself and/or the occasion, instead I use the frustration to push myself to find other ways to get involved and be an effective dad, role model, father figure.

(I don't think this next opinion is PC anymore, but you know what I mean)

Upsettingly, I will never be "the man of the house" and do any of the "typical dad stuff", putting toys together on Christmas Day, fixing things around the house, building stuff in the garden, showing kids how to repair their bikes. I just want someone to need me, be wanted incessantly, I want to be someone's everything – it terrifies me that this might become one of those 'unattainable aspirations.'

I might not be amazing at anything physical, but I can be an amazingly, reliable, helpful and supportive dad, I can help with the academic side, and life in general. Life now, is just about being the most loving, attentive, thoughtful, considerate, dad I can manage. A bit of a gap has developed between Alfie and me but, I'll always be here, "ready when you are Alf".

I recently bought a large tent (wheelchair size), and we go camping a handful of times a year. When we go camping or any trip that's no-more than a long-weekend, I spend the duration of the trip in my chair, not ideal but this way I am more of an active participant of whatever's going on. I always make sure I involve myself as much as I possibly can, ball games are tricky, but I always make sure I'm there and taking part – referee, goalkeeper, obstacle/defender, I'll get involved in any way possible, I'll do anything apart from just watching.

Outside of spending time with my boys, I travel around delivering road safety presentations in schools, colleges, universities, various armed forces barracks. It started with a couple a year for 1 single fire service, but at my busiest I did nearly 20 in a single year, shared between 3 different fire services, I speak/have spoken at events organized by either: Dorset and Wiltshire, Devon and Cornwall, or Bristol and Avon fire service. I've even presented at the MoD HQ in Whitehall, London, I will visit anywhere that'll have me.
I know, nothing will ever make up for the damage, caused by the crash in 2012 but, I will always do absolutely anything asked of me, so as the 2 dads that didn't make it, didn't die in vain. I'm not asking/I don't expect to be forgiven, that would be too much of an easy way out, I know I don't deserve to get off that easily. Considering this thought I won't let anything keep me down, I just need to keep banging the drum for road safety, mental strength, optimism and positivity in general.

In my life, I've been through my fair share of negative experiences, a few spontaneous and the rest self-inflicted. It's a concern that maybe life today, the endless guilt, the infinite shame, the lifelong inability to ever physically interact or embrace my loved ones, mightn't be enough of a price to pay. Chilling thoughts often grab me, regarding the apparent race I've found myself in, against the pace of my physical deterioration. Despite however valid this concern may be, I do my best to keep a positive mind set.

Since my accident I have grown up and matured considerably. Although unbelievably effective I wouldn't recommend the events that brought about this transformation.

> "If you always do what you've always done, you'll always get what you've always got"

If you are unhappy in life, constantly at odds with the world, endlessly finding problems, take a step back, you need to stop this way of processing life, you need to ask yourself some serious questions. I can't help with the questions – everyone's path will be different. Do your best to ensure your end goal is never too far from your thoughts as ultimately, it's about what **you** want from life. If you want to change your life/turn things around, it *can* be done, but having the sincere will to do so is essential.

> "If you don't leave your past in the past, it will destroy your future"

I used to get so wrapped up in dwelling on negatives, how poor my luck was, that I was on my own no one cared, and how nothing ever went my way, I've managed to stop this, it's simply wasting time and energy. I found that recognising what isn't helping, was the first step, then making changes came next for me, it won't be easy but, devote time to finding and focusing on next steps, being proactive and maintaining a positive mindset is critical.

> "A problem shared is a problem halved"

Growing up, I never gave any thought to positive thinking, beliefs or ideas, I didn't ever even consider mental health in general – I don't think many do? But, over the years since the crash, I've learnt 1st hand just how important it is for a person's overall wellbeing. Poor mental health can be your biggest obstacle in life, likewise it could also be your most helpful, powerful, beneficial asset.

A saying that I had to keep reminding myself of over the years when trying to better myself; "it's not the cards you're dealt, it's what you do with them", look at what I did/have done/am doing with mine. After finding and seeing everything from a more beneficial point of view, I've completely revitalised my mind, attitude and outlook on life. I feel truly blessed to have lived the life I have, gained such experience and to have been rewarded with my boys.
I am living breathing proof to anyone reading this book that every cloud, no matter how dark, daunting and ominous they may appear, they'll always be a silver lining, it mightn't be obvious or even easy to find, but stick with it, sometimes they just take time to show. Every negative *does indeed* have at least 1 positive, perspective is the key.

Yes, my boys and officially getting my capacity back are the biggest personal landmarks of my life to date, but it is nowhere near the end for me, I have plenty more ambitions to chase. I **will** create an income. This book **is** going to help me acquire a plush accessible campervan. I **will** manage to get myself on BBC's national morning news, next to their big red sofa. Jonathon Woss **is** going to invite me on his talk-show. Elon **is** going to consult me when Tesla fiiiinally get round to producing something wheelchair accessible, (Free of any financial fee to you Elon, just leave me with Neuralink for a bit)

"Don't fear failure, every mistake is a lesson to learn from"

For me, the crash and my own trauma that followed was a minor inconvenience, in my ambition to make "something" of myself. After an incredibly mild experience, I can tell you, it's not the "having" of stuff, time, money that brings happiness, satisfaction, fulfilment, those sorts of feelings, emotions and more, are all in the pursuit. I have always wanted to make something of myself, and I know I will, as long as I maintain my determined, proactive mind-set, I am positive I can and will. I will never be happy to simply exist in life – I **WILL** thrive! Watch this space.

"Shoot for the moon, you'll hit stars - even if you miss,"

Use negatives to fuel your ambitions, set that objective, see more, do more, believe in yourself, believe you can achieve your end goal, it can be done, you can do it. Confront your fears, never stop moving forward, keep progressing, keep on climbing life's ladder – you will be amazed at what you can achieve. Be kind, be considerate, be constructive, be mindful, but above all enjoy the ride, we only get 1 go round.

Accept, adapt, and overcome.

Instagram: ecpie24

TikTok: greg_sumner

Facebook: Is the driver sober?

X: gregsumner1990

LinkedIn: Greg Sumner

Printed in Great Britain
by Amazon